E/ESCWA/SDD/2015/4

**Economic and Social Commission for Western Asia**

# Population and Development Report
# Issue No. 7

## Overcoming Population Vulnerability to Water Scarcity in the Arab Region

**UNITED NATIONS**
Beirut

2

ISSN. 0255-5123
e-ISBN. 978-92-1-057622-2
Sales No. E.15.II.L.5

# Acknowledgements

This report was only possible through the dedicated leadership and guidance of Frederico Neto, Director of the Social Development Division of the United Nation's Economic and Social Commission for Western Asia (ESCWA), the overall supervision of Karima El Korri, Chief of the Population and Social Development Section (PSDS) and the direct coordination of Rouba Arja, First Population Affairs Officer, PSDS.

This publication is the product of the collaborative work among many ESCWA staff members including Rouba Arja, Lara El Khoury, Tala Harb, Jozef Bartovic, Raidan Al-Saqqaf and Paul Tacon, who all contributed to researching, drafting and reviewing various parts of the report.

The case studies were produced by Rima Habib, American University of Beirut, Lebanon, and Nedjma Koval, Chief Executive Officer of Integrated Services, Indigenous Solutions, Jordan. We would like to acknowledge their dedication and the high quality of their work.

Furthermore, we would like to acknowledge and thank the experts who participated in meetings to review the initial research and validate the report findings including Ayman Abouhadid, Ain Shams University, Egypt; Hala Abouali, Cairo University, Egypt; Raya Muttarak, International Institute for Applied Systems Analysis, Austria; Amer Salman, University of Jordan; Carol Chouchani Cherfane, Chief, Water Resources Section, ESCWA; Marwan Khawaja, Chief, Demographic and Social Statistics Section, ESCWA; and Mohammad Al-Hamdi, First Economic Affairs Officer, Food and Environment Policies Section, ESCWA.

Finally, our gratitude goes to the reviewers of the report, Abbas Elzein, University of Sydney, Australia, and Farzaneh Roudi, Population Reference Bureau, United States, for reviewing the report and providing valuable insights and feedback.

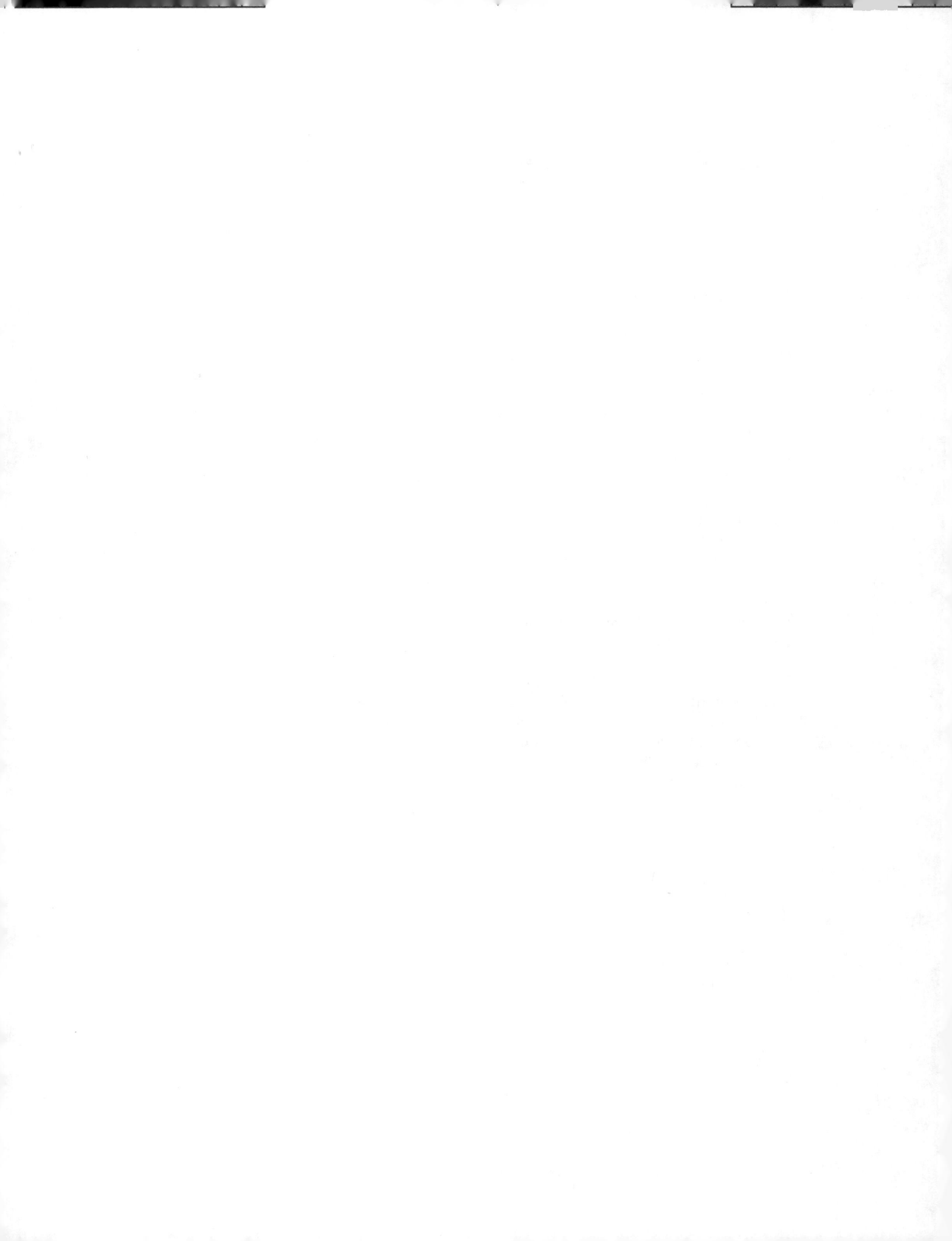

# Contents

**List of Maps**

**List of Boxes**

# Introduction

Environmental sustainability is one of the most prominent issues of the twenty-first century. Building the global 2030 Agenda for Sustainable Development around this important dimension reflects the level of concern and the urgent need to address environmental challenges to ensure that natural resources are protected and preserved for posterity. Against this backdrop, the vulnerability of the Arab region and its populations to water scarcity remains a key concern for individuals, communities and governments striving to achieve sustainable development and well-being for all citizens.[1]

Currently, the Arab region is facing major environmental challenges, including water pollution and chronic water shortages, long-term damage to ecosystems, air pollution, deforestation and land degradation. Environmental changes are affecting land coverage owing to increasing agricultural activities; diversification of land use, primarily towards tourism and mining activities; heavy deforestation; and rapid growth of urban areas.

Desertification, climate change, pollution and armed conflicts are resulting in grave degradation of natural resources. Air pollution leads to, among other consequences, the acidification of soils, lakes and streams, increasing health risks and causing damage to ecosystems. Losses in biodiversity as a consequence of overgrazing by domestic animals, overuse of land and water resources and overpopulation can also be observed across the region.[2] Alongside extractive industries, transportation and industrial activities are the main sources of air pollution in the region, which is further exacerbated by seasonal sand and dust storms that carry pollutants over long distances.[3] Coastal and marine areas are experiencing degradation owing to rapid coastal development, sea- and land-based pollution as well as overfishing.

However, considering the ever-increasing rate of depletion of water resources and the prospect of irreversible exhaustion of this natural resource, freshwater scarcity is the most significant environmental challenge in the Arab region. It is now recognized as the top environmental issue in 19 out of the 22 Arab countries, followed by desertification and land degradation, which significantly affects 17 Arab countries; and by pollution, a key environmental issue in 13 Arab countries.[4]

Population dynamics, if ignored, can contribute to unsustainable patterns of production and consumption and, as a consequence, to water scarcity. Population size, urbanization, migration and the changing age structure of populations are inherently linked to the environment, increasing both resource needs and the impacts on pollution made by individuals. For example, total renewable water resources per capita in the Arab region almost halved between 1982 and 2012, while the overall size of the population more than doubled over the same period. However, the relationship between population dynamics and environmental changes is not one that is clear-cut and linear. The environmental implications of population dynamics are determined by a complex interplay of a multitude of forces and factors, such as technology, political context and institutional and governance frameworks. Similarly, with water being a vital resource that influences population health, livelihoods and socioeconomic resilience, the implications of water scarcity on population are significant and affected by a set of interconnected factors. As the global population continues to grow, limits on such resources as water have come into sharp focus and these complex relationships have to be examined carefully.

Indeed, this report endeavours to analyse the nexus between population dynamics and water scarcity, and to provide recommendations on how to improve policies and programmes addressing water scarcity in order to reduce the vulnerability of particular population groups and enhance resilience of populations at risk. The report looks at water scarcity through a population lens in order to enable policymakers and governments to develop targeted and people-centred policies and programmes to tackle water scarcity issues and to address its differential impact on specific population groups which might be more vulnerable to and less capable of coping with water scarcity.

Chapter I introduces the report's thematic focus: the nexus between water scarcity and population dynamics. It sets the scene by describing the extent of water scarcity in the Arab region and explains the rationale for developing population-centred policies that place the needs and rights of all people at the core of efforts to address water scarcity issues in the region. It also highlights the mutually reinforcing relationship by demonstrating how population dynamics are themselves affected by water availability, quality and water use tendencies.[5] It presents a strong case for fully integrating population dynamics into sustainable development policies and, more specifically, into efforts aimed at combating water scarcity, which in turn could reduce population vulnerability to water scarcity and increase its resilience.

Chapter II is built on the premise that water scarcity and population dynamics cut through all three pillars of sustainable development. It defines the concept of vulnerability to water scarcity by taking into consideration the three components of sustainable development, and argues that sustainable development presents a relevant framework to address population vulnerability to water scarcity. The chapter explains how the exposure and resilience components of vulnerability are linked to the economic, environmental and social pillars of sustainable development, and what factors can reduce vulnerability and resilience of specific population groups, including the political context. It further argues that water scarcity as a specific environmental stressor can have a differentiated impact on different population groups, highlighting the role of various factors, including age, gender, socioeconomic status, mobility and place of residence.

The analysis in chapter III is based on selected case studies in three geographical locations, namely: Sana'a in Yemen as well as the Jordan River Valley and Mafraq in Jordan. By using population sub-groups as units of study, it demonstrates the differential impact of water scarcity on subgroups within a specific socioeconomic context. Building on the nexus between population dynamics and water scarcity (as explored in chapter I), and considering the factors that could reduce or increase vulnerability and resilience (as described in chapter II), the case studies presented in this chapter deepen the understanding of exposure and resilience of these groups in their specific socioeconomic context and geographic setting. It concludes by proposing measures to mitigate the negative impacts of water scarcity and by drawing policy recommendations for enhancing the resilience of populations at risk, identifying measures that are not universal but relevant and tailored to a specific group of concern.

# I. Nexus between Population Dynamics and Water Scarcity

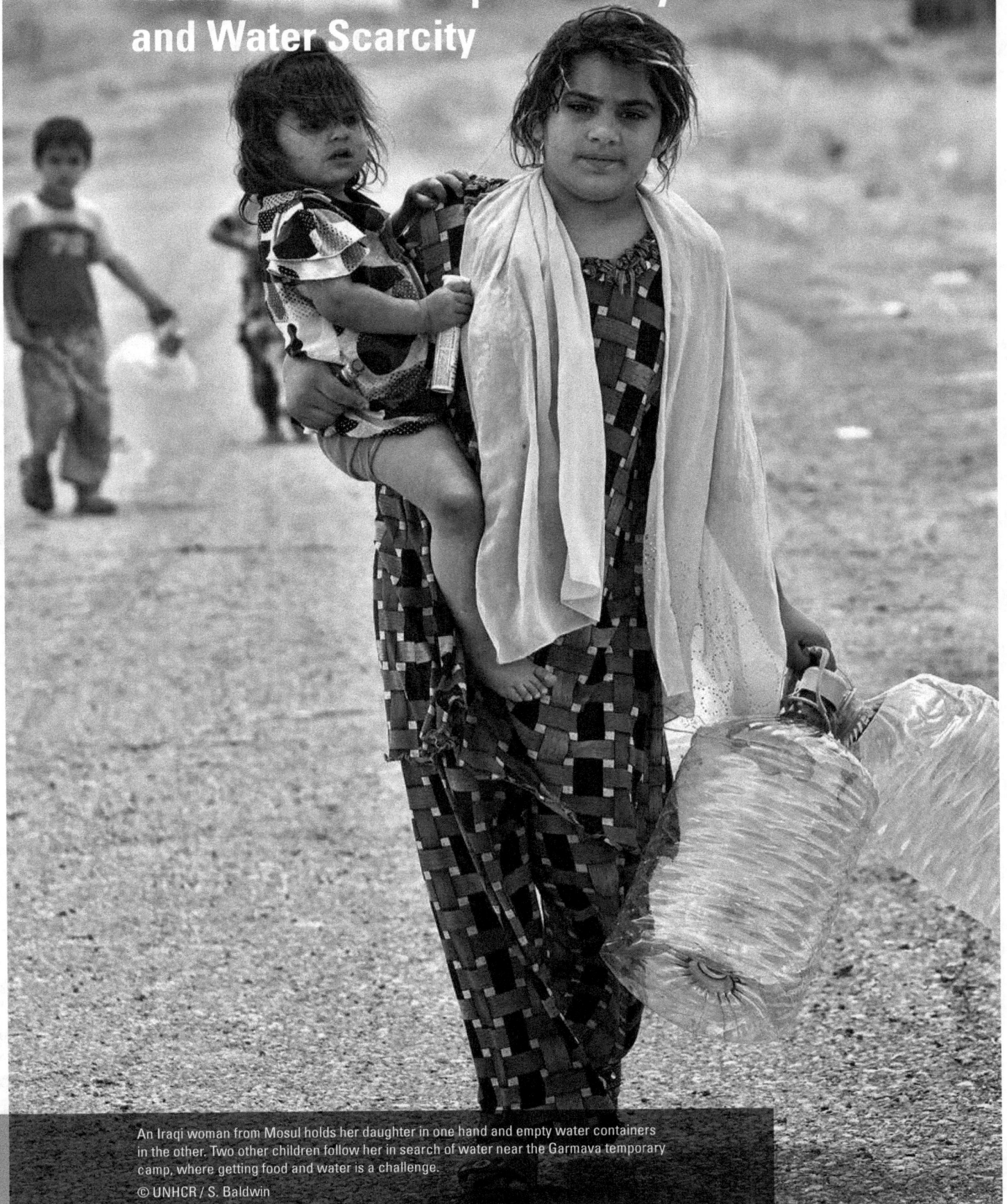

An Iraqi woman from Mosul holds her daughter in one hand and empty water containers in the other. Two other children follow her in search of water near the Garmava temporary camp, where getting food and water is a challenge.

© UNHCR / S. Baldwin

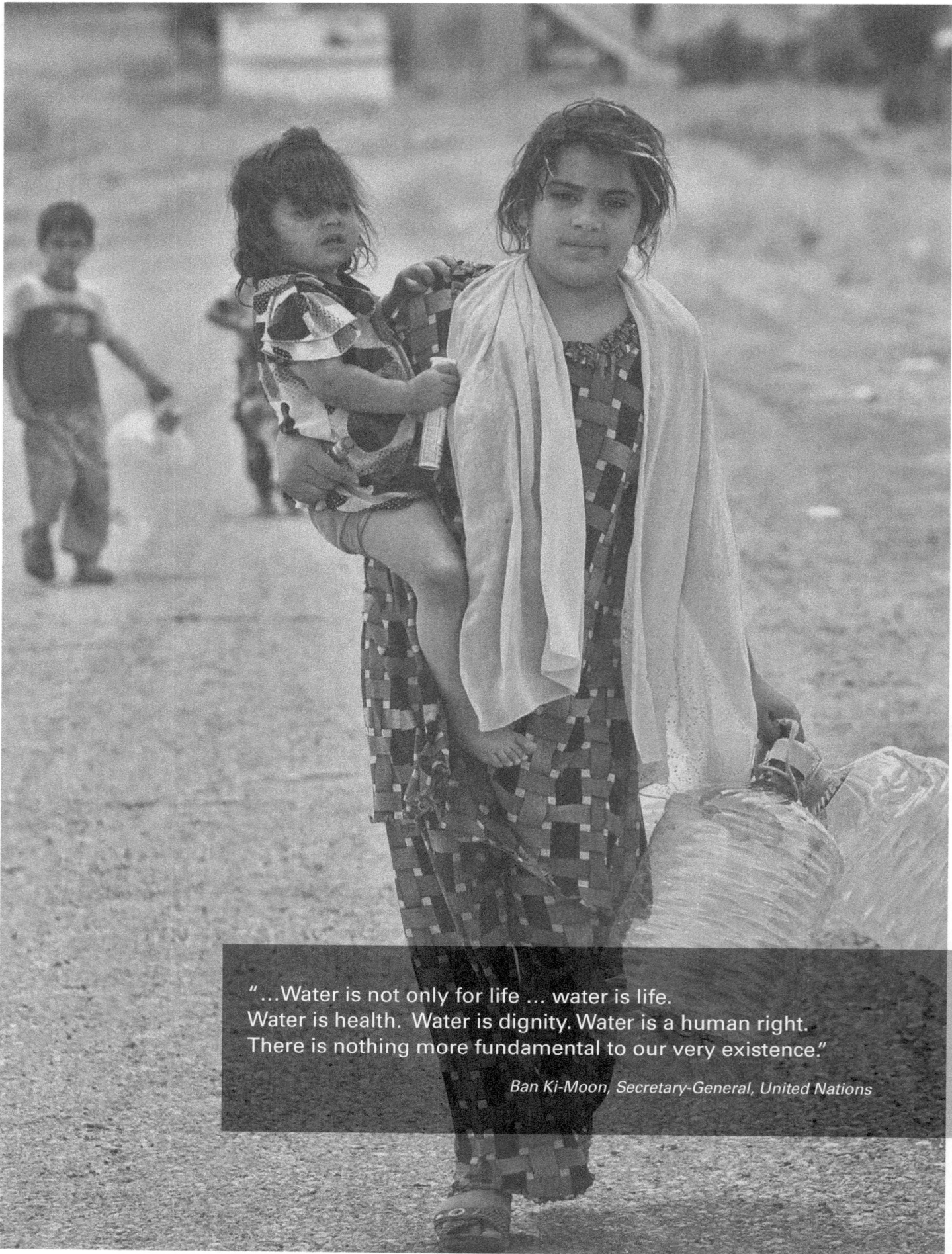

"…Water is not only for life … water is life.
Water is health.  Water is dignity. Water is a human right.
There is nothing more fundamental to our very existence."

*Ban Ki-Moon, Secretary-General, United Nations*

# I. Nexus between Population Dynamics and Water Scarcity

## A. Population dynamics in the Arab region

The population dynamics in the region, namely, population size, urbanization levels, age structures, and internal and international migration flows, are significantly expanding the region's water demand. Population dynamics have witnessed considerable changes in the past three decades as the region's population size more than doubled and is still projected to increase further by two-thirds by 2050 (figure 1). The significant population growth is accompanied by notable changes in the lifestyle of people who are rapidly urbanizing and moving away from their traditional way of living which was more adapted to the environmental specificities of the region. The number of urban dwellers in the region more than doubled between 1985 and 2010, further increasing pressure on the environment (figure 2). Population growth leads to the spread of unsustainable practices in agricultural activities and exerts pressure on already scarce freshwater resources. Furthermore, water scarcity is occurring in the challenging contexts of Arab countries facing major social, economic and political transitions, conflicts and unprecedented flows of refugees and internally displaced persons (IDPs), thereby posing new challenges to sustainable development.

Despite country heterogeneity, the following four figures provide an overview of the population dynamics in the region: growing population, increase in the number of urban dwellers, changes in age structure of the population with a growing working age group, and an increase in the number of international migrants in the region.

**Figure 1.** Population growth predictions for the Arab region, 2012 and 2050

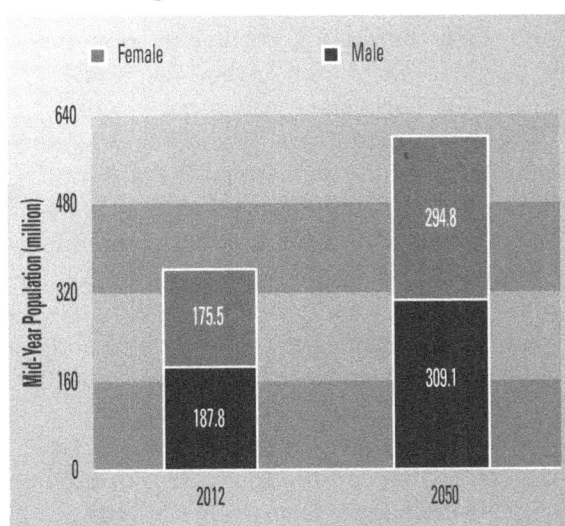

Source: ESCWA, *The Demographic Profile of the Arab Countries* (2014).

**Figure 2.** Urban and rural population of the Arab region, 1980-2050

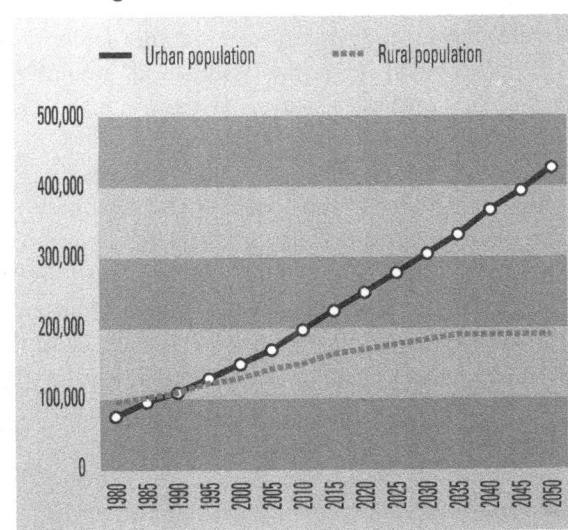

Source: ESCWA, *The Demographic Profile of the Arab Countries* (2014).

**Figure 3.** Population pyramid of the Arab region, 2010

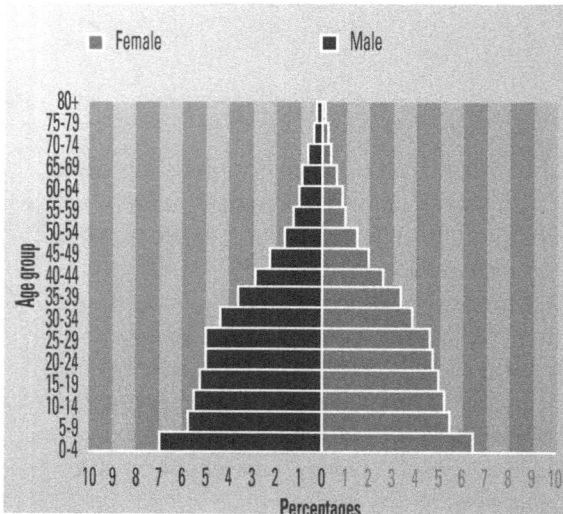

Source: ESCWA, *The Demographic Profile of the Arab Countries* (2014).

**Figure 4.** International migrant stock of the Arab region, 1990-2013

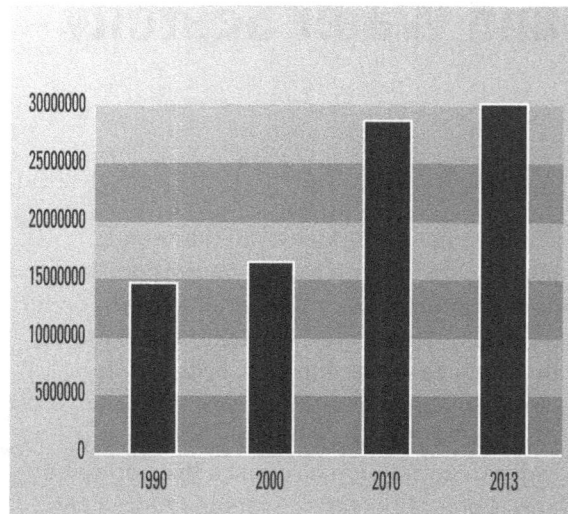

Source: ESCWA, *The Demographic Profile of the Arab Countries* (2014).

## B. Water scarcity in the Arab region

The Arab region is the most water-scarce region worldwide, with seven Arab countries in the global top ten of most water-scarce nations.[1] A wide array of factors is further challenging this physical scarcity.

Agriculture remains the largest consumer of freshwater in the Arab countries. Inefficient irrigation causes significant losses of available water resources, estimated at around 60 per cent in some areas.[2] Uncontrolled and excessive use of fertilizers and pesticides causes soil contamination, thereby seriously threatening groundwater quality with potential leakages into aquifers.[3] In Gaza, for example, nitrate levels in drinking water, which have harmful effects on health, have risen to around 600-800 mg/litre as a result of agricultural and wastewater pollution, while the maximum tolerable limit is 50 mg/litre. Tunisia, where nitrate concentrations have reached around 800 mg/litre, is also facing similar concerns.[4] Sometimes, the need for energy to ensure access to water causes an overexploitation

of other resources and an increase in waste generation. This occurs, for example, when farmers are encouraged to employ oversized engines and industries to invest in water systems and power backup to extract water.[5]

Industrial waste, domestic sewage and agricultural (mostly untreated) return flows are also often discharged into water channels and lakes, thereby raising health concerns of populations of many Arab countries. In Egypt, discharges are, to a great extent, loaded with contaminants and bacteria, toxic chemicals and heavy metals. In the Sudan, the heavy contaminations of surface waters impede efforts of water management and treatment, and result in the deterioration of the country's water quality, leading to insufficient supplies of potable water and causing health concerns.[6]

Similar to prevailing unsustainable practices, inappropriate governance systems negatively affect water supply in terms of both the quantity of available water and its quality, putting additional burden on this scarce resource. While the water situation in the Arab region requires urgent attention and efficient management, several factors hinder Arab governments from making progress in water governance, including unclear or overlapping responsibilities, lack of funding, inefficient institutional mechanisms, lack of public awareness, centralized decision-making and inadequate enforcement structures.[7] Inefficient water governance and inadequate management fail to address water sustainability. These governance shortcomings represent additional challenges to tackling water scarcity. The main deadlock that decision makers and government officials are facing is caused by the lack of water policy reform. Most Arab countries deal with water management problems in silos and, therefore, water is often not considered as an integral part of economic and social sectors. Water and energy resources, while interrelated and interdependent, are separately managed by different institutions that do not necessarily share common interests, thereby weakening effective water governance and leading to water overexploitation. It is important to note that increasing competition between the sectors necessitates integrated responses to ensure that all needs are met in an adequate and sustainable way.

Moreover, most countries in the Arab region find themselves unable to fund investments in water source solutions or treatment of wastewater. Given the large-scale investments needed to pay for the costs of maintaining, developing and expanding water infrastructure, financial gaps further weaken governance patterns in the region.

Treating municipal wastewater represents one of the solutions to meet a substantial share of the escalating water demand in Arab countries, given that it can provide an alternative source. However, countries often face several social, technical, institutional and political barriers to expanding their water treatment and reuse facilities. For example,

in Jordan, 100 per cent of treated municipal wastewater quantities are reused for irrigation, whereas in Palestine, 80 per cent of treated municipal wastewater quantities are discharged to the sea.[8] Overall, most countries of the region have programmes for the treatment and reuse of wastewater, but they lack clear and efficient institutional guidelines on its regulation.[9] Furthermore, treatment processes and infrastructure capacities in most Arab countries have resulted in an ineffective treatment of municipal wastewater, with the rates of treated wastewater varying from country to country. For example, in Iraq, 67 per cent of municipal wastewater collected by sewer piped networks are secondary treated, whereas in Bahrain, 100 per cent of municipal wastewater collected by sewer piped networks are tertiary treated.[10]

The above-mentioned challenges are exacerbated by negative economic, social and political conditions as well as by persistent conflicts and instability. These conditions limit the capacities of Arab countries to take measures aimed at addressing effectively water-related challenges and, indeed, they have in some cases made the challenges more acute.

## C. Nexus between population dynamics and water scarcity

The region's water scarcity, stemming from the endemic aridity of the region, is further exacerbated by a myriad of other factors, including population dynamics. As demonstrated in this chapter, population dynamics influence and shape "the scale and scope of development challenges and ... the achievement of sustainable development and poverty eradication".[11] They must be accounted for in drawing development plans and strategies given their potential to impact the achievement of economic development that is socially inclusive and environmentally sustainable.

By influencing the levels of consumption and availability of natural resources, population dynamics affect environmental sustainability.[12] Conversely, population dynamics are strongly affected by the level of social, economic and environmental development.

This interrelationship between population dynamics and sustainable development has received increasing levels of attention from the international community. It is recognized in principle 6 of the Programme of Action of the International Conference on Population and Development (box 1), and in principle 8 of the Rio Declaration, which underlines the importance of promoting sustainable production and consumption patterns. This

interconnectedness was again reiterated in paragraphs 21 and 144 of the Rio+20 outcome document.[13]

Further to United Nations resolution 64/292 of 2010 that explicitly recognizes the human right to water and sanitation and acknowledges that clean drinking water and sanitation are crucial to the realization of all human rights, the Rio+20 document also focuses on a rights-based approach to water for all: "We reaffirm our commitments regarding the human right to safe drinking water and sanitation, to be progressively realized for our populations, with full respect for national sovereignty. We also highlight our commitment to the International Decade for Action, "Water for Life", 2005-2015".[14]

**Box 1.** International Conference on Population and Development and water scarcity

The 1994 Programme of Action of the International Conference on Population and Development (ICPD) was the first internationally agreed development framework to highlight the differentiated impact of the growing scarcity of water on various population groups. This issue was addressed in chapter three of the Programme of Action, which emphasized the interrelationships between population and sustainable development. The Programme of Action included several proposals to address this issue, including integrating demographic factors into environmental impact assessments; improving planning and decision-making processes aimed at achieving sustainable development; and using demographic data to promote sustainable resource management, especially of ecologically fragile systems.[a]

The 20-year review of the implementation of the ICPD Programme of Action in Arab countries revealed that while 16 out of 19 respondent countries had taken action to promote environmental resource management, only ten countries had undertaken concrete action targeting the needs of people living within or on the edge of fragile ecosystems. Furthermore, six out of these ten countries described progress as deficient or behind schedule.[b]

The 2013 Cairo Declaration, emerging from the 20-year review of the ICPD for Arab States, carried renewed emphasis on this dynamic in recognition of the interaction between population and the environment to achieve sustainable development and water and food security. The declaration specifically stated that regional and local climate change response measures needed to take into account the distribution, vulnerability and resilience of the targeted populations.[c]

[a] United Nations Population Fund (UNFPA), Programme of Action: Adopted at the International Conference on Population and Development (2004).
[b] ESCWA, League of Arab States, Economic Commission for Africa and UNFPA, Development Challenges and Population Dynamics in a Changing Arab World: Cairo Declaration (Cairo, 2013). Available from www.unfpa.org/sites/default/files/event-pdf/Cairo_Declaration_English.pdf.
[c] ESCWA, League of Arab States, Economic Commission for Africa and UNFPA, ICPD Beyond 2014 Arab States Report: Development Challenges and Population Dynamics in a Changing Arab World, Executive Summary (Cairo, 2014).

**Figure 5.** Relationship between population dynamics and water availability

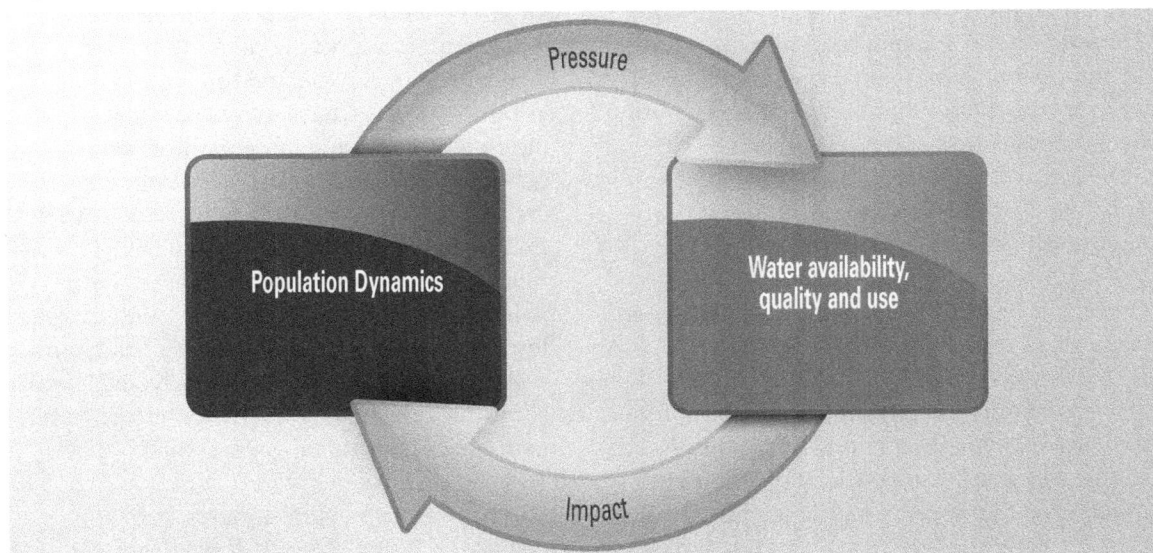

**Source:** Prepared by ESCWA.

States and international organizations need to provide financial resources, assist in capacity-building and technology transfer to help countries, particularly developing countries, to provide safe, clean, accessible and affordable drinking water and sanitation for all. Obligations stemming from these documents require States to protect and fulfil this right, ensuring access for all to a sufficient amount of safe drinking water for personal and domestic use, and to ensure access to adequate sanitation as a basic constituent of human dignity.

This relationship between water scarcity and population dynamics is mutually reinforcing. The examination of the impact of water scarcity on population leads to complex and multifaceted linkages that can hardly be structured in a linear causal relationship. Adequate water supply and quality are important for the functioning, growth and prosperity of all economic sectors and, consequently, impacts the well-being and livelihoods of populations. Water supply and quality also have a direct impact on the movement of populations, including rural to urban migration and international migration, on the stability of countries and their relationships, and on population health.

In order for countries to be able to attend to the needs of current and future generations and advance their well-being, information on the size and growth rate of the population as well as on the population's geographic distribution and age structure at present and in the near future is needed. Failure to properly account for population dynamics and trends in the development planning process will result in policies and programmes that are neither well-informed nor adequate. This is because population dynamics are continuously changing, and are shaping and being shaped by economic growth and development, which affect production, employment creation, income distribution and poverty reduction; and by spending on social protection schemes, including pensions. Population dynamics are also influencing and being influenced by the availability and accessibility of health, education, housing, sanitation and water, food and energy facilities and services.[15]

Nevertheless, efforts to advance economic and social progress "for a large and growing ... population will place mounting pressures on the planet's finite resources, challenging environmental sustainability and contributing to climate change and natural disasters".[16] Thus, efforts must be made to ensure that economic and social advancements do not endanger environmental sustainability.

Given the fundamental relationship between population dynamics and such existing key development challenges as poverty eradication and environmental sustainability, and the influence they have on addressing these challenges and on achieving development objectives, this section examines further how population dynamics affect sustainable development, with a particular emphasis on water resources. It also discusses how water, in turn, affects population dynamics.

## 1. Population size and growth

The population dynamics in the region, namely, its population growth, urbanization, changing age structure and migration flows, are significantly expanding water demand. The size of the Arab population was 363 million in 2012 and is projected to reach 488 million by 2030. The Arab region will continue to experience high population growth rates well into 2030. The projected average annual population growth rate for the region for the periods 2010-2015 and 2025-2030 stands at 2.00 per cent and 1.37 per cent, respectively, compared to a global average annual growth rate of 1.15 per cent and 0.83 per cent for the same periods. Growth rates are expected to be among the highest in Arab least developed countries (LDCs), including the Comoros, Mauritania, the Sudan and Yemen; and in countries affected by conflict and ongoing crises, such as Iraq, Palestine and Somalia. While fertility rates are decreasing in the region (from 6.3 children per woman in 1980-1985 to 3.2 children for the period 2010-2015), they still remain above the world average (2.5 children per woman).[17]

The impact of population growth on water availability in Arab countries will be considerable, especially given that most of this growth is expected to take place in countries that are already water stressed,[18] and that do not have the economic and technological capacities to deal with the ensuing challenges.[19] In fact, most countries in the Middle East and North Africa cannot meet their current water demand.[20] This situation will be exacerbated as population growth increases demand for water at all levels of society and in all sectors (agriculture, industry, etc.), which will further increase the stress on freshwater resources and reduce water availability.

Renewable freshwater resources present a basis for measuring water scarcity, with the most frequently used measure being the amount of annual per-capita freshwater availability within national boundaries. Population growth reduces the amount of water available per capita and affects water stress and scarcity.[21] Estimates show that population growth in the region between 1982 and 2012 contributed to a reduction of almost 50 per cent in the average amount of total water resource per capita (figure 6).

One of the biggest challenges of our time centres on meeting the needs of a large and growing population in a sustainable manner in order to preserve the environment. Unsustainable and inequitable patterns of consumption, mostly in developed countries, are causing significant environmental degradation, negatively affecting the lives of many poor people.[22] Feeding the growing number of people is set to entail an increase in both agricultural production and productivity. Production of other important goods and services at a larger scale will also be required, putting additional strain on natural resources, increasingly affecting water, energy, forests, land and climate.[23] Moreover, high rates of population growth in developing countries tend to outstrip investments in such basic services as health and education, thereby weakening

**Figure 6.** Population growth and freshwater resource availability in the Arab region, 1982-2012

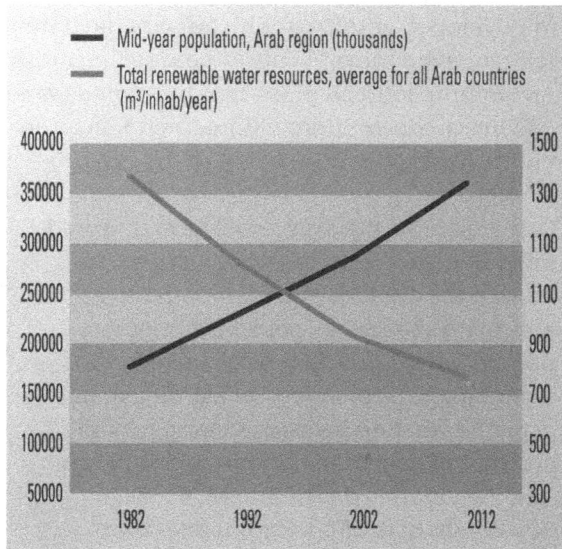

— Mid-year population, Arab region (thousands)
— Total renewable water resources, average for all Arab countries (m³/inhab/year)

Sources: FAO, Aquastat, 2014, available from www.fao.org/nr/water/aquastat/data/query/; and ESCWA, *The Demographic Profile of the Arab Countries* (2013).

poverty alleviation efforts and prospects for economic growth. As such, preserving the environment necessitates addressing population growth factors, vigorously encouraging sustainable patterns of production and consumption, and working towards achieving green and equitable economic growth. This will help to slow down the depletion of non-renewable resources and increase the per-capita availability of renewable ones, thereby reducing pressure on the environment.

Globally, agriculture accounts for about 70 per cent of global water use. Around 95 per cent of water use in countries with agricultural-based economies is consumed by this sector.[24] The situation is no different in the Arab region, where agriculture represents the bulk of the demand for water. Irrigated land in the region almost doubled between 1965 and 1997, owing partly to increases in food demand in line with population growth.[25] Meeting this increase in food demand translates into using greater quantities of water and into more agricultural production, thereby further increasing pressure on water resources.[26] Other sectors of the economy also increase the demand for water albeit to a lesser extent. In the majority of countries, households account for a small share of overall water use, with the exception of such countries as Kuwait that do not rely on agriculture or industry. "While demand for water in all sectors has increased rapidly, it is increasing most quickly at the domestic level".[27] Growing populations combined with such factors as higher per-capita income, urbanization and improved water accessibility have increased household demand for water.[28]

## 2. Age structure

Notwithstanding regional variations, Arab countries have a relatively young age structure. In 2010, a total of 33 per cent of the Arab population was aged under 14, and 20 per cent was aged 15-24.[29] Projections show that these percentages will decrease by 2030 to 27.8 per cent and 17.5 per cent, respectively; and that this downward trend will persist until 2050 when these proportions are expected to reach 23 per cent and 15 per cent for the respective age groups. In 2010, the working age population (25-60) formed the largest age group of the Arab population, at 43 per cent, with projections showing that it will remain the largest age group, making up 49 per cent of the population in 2030 and 50 per cent by 2050. The smallest age group is that of older persons (aged 65 or over), which represented 4 per cent of the population in 2010 and is projected to increase to 6 per cent in 2030. The pace of the increase will pick up after 2030 and the proportion of older persons is expected to reach 12 per cent of the Arab population by 2050.

Different age groups have diverse requirements and expectations; and the changing age structures present both opportunities and challenges for sustainable development. A fall in fertility levels and slower population growth rates will result in an increase in the proportion of people in the working-age group, compared to the dependent-age groups. This situation can, for a while, create a demographic window of opportunity that is conducive to economic growth and has a positive impact on development. Nevertheless, to reap the demographic dividend, countries will have to promote an enabling environment by formulating policies that increase investment, create jobs for the enlarged labour force and support human capital development.[30]

The transition from high to low levels of fertility and the continuing increase in life expectancy will result in ageing populations. This will create significant challenges associated with improving health-care systems to cater for the medical needs of older persons and social insurance schemes, including pension systems, and to ensure the well-being and dignity of older persons. The ageing phenomenon can also present opportunities for the social and economic development of countries, "provided that older persons benefit from good health, and that they have economic security, and are empowered to actively participate in economic, social and political life".[31]

The changing structure of different age groups has significant implications for water use. Specifically, an increasing share of the working-age population will create challenges in terms of employment, public expenditure, migration and housing; and translates into an increase in consumption and production, which entails the use of more freshwater resources. Experience from countries where consumption and production patterns have changed with changing age structures shows that a larger working-age group that drives economic activity generates an increase in water demand. Living longer involves greater use and, therefore, a greater production of medicines and the establishment of more medical and health-care services. Additionally,

a more global economy, modern lifestyles and communications technology enhance the exposure of young people and drive those "in developing countries to want more and those in developed countries who already have more to want even more".[32] This increases the stress on water resources given that per-capita water use increases with growing demand, income and consumption.[33]

Consequently, the right environment would need to be in place to enable harnessing these opportunities and addressing the emerging challenges posed by different population groups. In the case of a large working-age population, investment in human capital formation is needed along with the creation of decent job opportunities to bring about economic development. Economic development is often accompanied with increased use of natural resources. Within the context of an ageing population, it becomes vital to ensure the right social protection and pension schemes that raise living standards and reduce poverty, and to put in place the adequate infrastructure that caters for the needs of older persons. In both situations, taking the necessary measures will exert additional pressure on natural resources, thereby straining the environment and increasing the threat of climate change. As such, in order to ensure sustainable development in all its three dimensions – social, economic and environmental – and advance the well-being of the population, there is a crucial need to build sustainable green economies and jobs and to promote sustainable patterns of consumption and production.

## 3. Urbanization

More than half of the Arab population resides in urban areas. In 2014, the percentage of urban dwellers stood at 58 per cent and is projected to reach 62 per cent by 2030 and 69 per cent by 2050.[34] The number of urban dwellers in the Arab region has more than doubled over the past three decades, reaching a total of 218.2 million in 2014. The majority of the region's population already resides in urban areas, with the percentage of urban dwellers estimated at 58 per cent in 2014, compared to a world average of 54 per cent. The regional average urban growth rate, which stood at 2.98 per cent per year for the period 2005-2010, is projected to decrease to 1.86 per cent for the period 2025-2030. Nevertheless, the region's urban population is projected to increase by 107.2 million persons between 2010 and 2030, rising from 196.8 million to 304.0 million. By 2050, it will account for more than two-thirds of the region's population. Estimates show that in 2014, the most urbanized countries in the region were Qatar, with 99 per cent of its population residing in urban areas, followed by Kuwait (98 per cent), Bahrain (89 per cent), Lebanon (88 per cent) and United Arab Emirates (85 per cent); and the least urbanized countries were the Comoros (28 per cent), the Sudan and Yemen (34 per cent), Somalia (39 per cent) and Egypt (43 per cent).

Population distribution also influences increases in domestic and municipal water demand and use, owing mainly to population growth in urban areas.[35] Cities in the Arab region are growing at a faster rate than countries as a whole. The average annual urban growth rate for the Arab region during the period 1980-1985 stood at 4.25 per cent, compared to an average regional population growth rate of 2.96 per cent for the same period. Projections show that the regional average annual urban growth rate for the period 2010-2015 will remain higher than the regional average annual population growth rate, standing at 2.54 per cent and 2.0 per cent, respectively, with both averages decreasing to 1.39 per cent and 0.89 per cent for the period 2045-2050. The above-mentioned dynamics will have an impact on achieving Sustainable Development Goal 11 of the 2030 Agenda for Sustainable Development that aims to make cities and human settlements inclusive, safe, resilient and sustainable; and to achieve, by 2030, inclusive and sustainable urbanization,

and reduce the adverse per-capita environmental impact of cities, including special attention to air quality, municipal and other waste management.

Urbanization is usually driven by natural internal urban population growth, rural-urban migration and annexation (expansion of urban areas by adding peripheral land).[36] Moreover, the considerably lower urban mortality of today's developing countries is another factor associated with urban congestion.[37] In such cases where urbanization is well planned and integrated in development strategies and plans, it can present significant opportunities for sustainable development. The Rio+20 outcome document stipulates that "well-planned and developed .... cities can promote economically, socially and environmentally sustainable societies".[38] This can be attributed to a number of factors, including the potential to benefit from economies of scale in the delivery of necessary services and infrastructure, providing them at a lower per capita cost owing to higher population density.[39] There is also potential to save energy, mainly in the housing and transportation sectors, given that urban dwellers tend to use less energy with consumption patterns that entail lower levels of greenhouse gas emissions. However, cities provide improved access to such services as education, health and housing and increased productive employment opportunities,[40] all of which could result in increased consumption levels as lifestyles change. This places an emphasis on adopting patterns of consumption and production that promote sustainability. The position of cities as drivers of sustainable development could be further enhanced by strengthening rural-urban linkages through integrated planning, thereby increasing the access of rural people to essential social services and economic opportunities.[41]

Indeed, if urban growth is inadequately planned, it could prove to be "environmentally and economically inefficient",[42] intensifying vulnerability to natural disasters and aggravating urban poverty. This in turn could hamper access to economic opportunities, quality infrastructure, housing and social services. Instead, the escalation of informal settlements and expansion of slum areas where dwellers are more exposed to extreme weather events will occur, putting additional pressure on already inadequate infrastructure and exacerbating vulnerability to environmental degradation and water scarcity. This could also result in a greater urban sprawl, bringing about inefficient land use and resource consumption patterns.[43]

In addition to the above-mentioned factors driving rural migration, a shortage of water resources and natural hazards, especially in areas where people depend on the availability of natural resources for survival, can push people to migrate from rural to urban areas. This could result in a considerable increase in the number of people residing in vulnerable urban and coastal areas and informal settings.[44] Residents of informal urban settings do not have adequate access to safe drinking water and sanitation services, which increases the risk of water contamination and associated illnesses.[45] Moreover, rapid urbanization can obstruct the development of suitable water infrastructure systems in cities, adequate sewage systems, distribution systems and regulatory mechanisms.[46] Thus, unplanned migration patterns put strain on water resources in ever-growing cities (see the impact of water scarcity on rural-to-urban migrants in Sana'a in chapter III).

Pressure on water sources mounts with urbanization mainly as a result of the presence of a considerable share of young people in urban areas who usually push for economic growth.[47] Higher concentrations of people in one area, increased population density and higher living standards increase water consumption. "Overall, the amount of water each person uses is expected to increase as incomes grow and consumption increases."[48] Consequently, "the gap between water supply and demand, estimated at more than 43 cubic kilometres a year in 2009, is expected to reach 127 cubic kilometres a year by 2020-2030".[49] However, at the same time, higher population density could "enable communities to invest in more efficient and cost-effective water management".[50]

Impervious surfaces are another issue connected with urbanization, which prevent the infiltration of water from rain and snow into the soil. Such surfaces increase the water flow speed, bringing pollutants into receiving water systems, thereby contaminating water and damaging its quality. They also increase the incidence of flash floods and, consequently, the occurrence of fatalities and damage to the infrastructure.[51]

## 4. International migration, refugee movements and internal displacement

International migrants formed 8.2 per cent of the region's total population in 2013, representing an increase of 2 per cent from 6.2 per cent in 1990. In absolute terms, this equates to a total of 30.3 million international migrants in 2013, double the figure of 14.9 million migrants in 1990.[52] The most prominent form of migration in the region is labour migration, with the largest stock of international migrants hosted by countries of the Gulf Cooperation Council (GCC). This subregion accounted for more than 22.3 million migrants in 2013 (73.8 per cent of the total international migrant stock in the region).

Forced migration and refugee flows are the second most prominent form of population movement in the region. In addition to the historic Palestinian refugee population hosted by Arab countries and the more recent influx of refugees from Iraq, the crisis in the Syrian Arab Republic has caused an unprecedented influx of refugees to neighbouring countries over the past few years. At the time of writing, a total of 4 million refugees had fled the Syrian Arab Republic since the beginning of the crisis.[53] The total number of Syrian refugees in Lebanon and Jordan alone amounts to approximately 1.2 million and 627,000, respectively.[54] Moreover, an increase in the occurrence of forced migration resulting from climate change and extreme weather conditions is expected in the future.[55] This is set to put additional pressure on the limited resources and infrastructure of host countries, many of which are middle-income and developing countries, challenging their capacity to adequately meet the needs and fulfil the rights of displaced populations. Numbers of IDPs are equally alarming, with 7.6 million IDPs in the Syrian Arab Republic alone, almost 3.3 million in Iraq, 3.1 million in the Sudan and 400,000 in Libya. The Arab region has the highest number of IDPs worldwide.[56]

It is important to note that, in many cases, "migrants move to areas where they are more vulnerable to natural hazards than in their countries of origin".[57] When migration takes place on a large scale, it has significant effects on both the country of destination and of origin.[58] Migration and water have a two-way relationship whereby migration affects and adds to water stress, and the decision to migrate can be affected by such stressors as water scarcity and flooding. The decision to migrate is also driven by the prevailing socioeconomic environment. Consequently, the pressure on water resources and on existing infrastructure will increase in countries of destination, further exacerbating the pressure on the environment. At the same time, such movements could diminish pressures on the vacated land, increasing the chances for the recovery of ecosystems.

With conflict and droughts cited as some of the major drivers of forced migration and urbanization, it comes as no surprise that the vast majority of those displaced in the Arab region currently do not reside in refugee camps, but rather in urban settings.[59] The displaced populations often reside in underserved and underdeveloped areas, exacerbating pre-existing vulnerabilities related to displacement, social and legal discrimination, and poverty (see the case study of al-Mafraq in chapter III). The absorption of forced migrants into towns and cities poses logistical quandaries in terms of targeting and ensuring the effective delivery and impact of appropriate assistance, including the provision of safe drinking water.

While the environmental impacts of refugee flows and internal displacement are difficult to separate from pre-existing environmental issues, many of which result from inappropriate government policies, unsustainable humanitarian assistance and mismanaged development assistance, cities in the region have undergone major socioeconomic transformations by absorbing millions of refugees. Sudden and forced population movements come at the expense of urban planning in many Arab cities, resulting in a proliferation of substandard housing and the emergence of unsafe slum settlements where residents may be without access to safe drinking water. With rising demand come price hikes, which carry particularly adverse effects for those displaced, as well as the urban poor, who struggle to afford the cost of food and water, utilities and housing. Furthermore, these crises and population movements also generate additional waste, which poses further threats to environmental sustainability and water quality.

# Factors Impacting Vulnerability to Water Scarcity

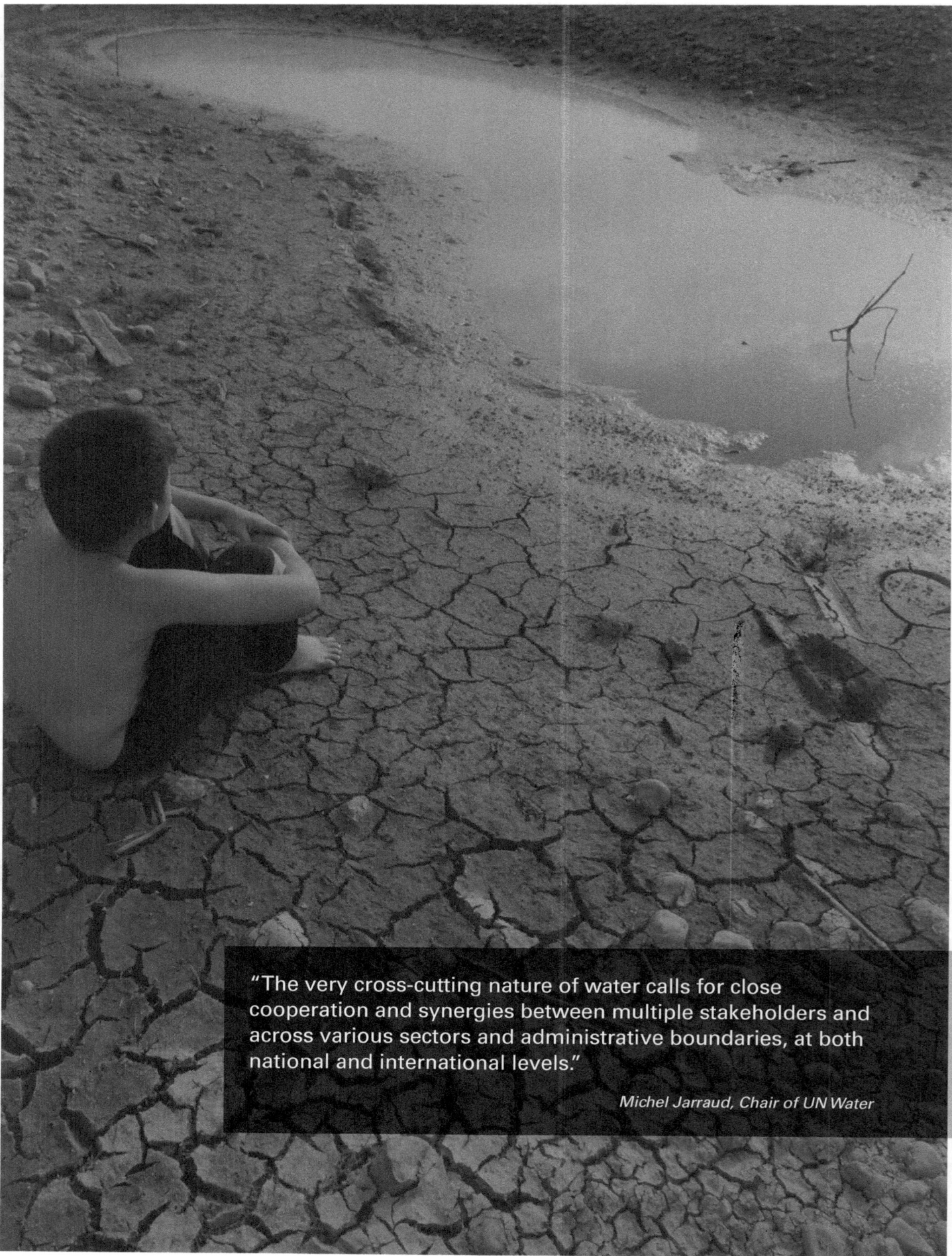

"The very cross-cutting nature of water calls for close cooperation and synergies between multiple stakeholders and across various sectors and administrative boundaries, at both national and international levels."

*Michel Jarraud, Chair of UN Water*

# II. Factors Impacting Vulnerability to Water Scarcity

## A. Vulnerability to water scarcity in the context of sustainable development

The three pillars of development – social, economic and environmental – form a nexus. In order for this nexus to be sustainable, a more equitable distribution of resources and a move towards a green economy with sustainable consumption and production patterns are essential.[1] To achieve this, development policies, including policies addressing water scarcity, should give due consideration to all three pillars of sustainable development. This approach was promulgated for the first time by the United Nations Conference on Environment and Development held in 1992. Subsequently, it became an overarching developmental principle that underpinned the approach of the International Conference on Population and Development held in 1994, the World Summit for Social Development in 1995, the Millennium Summit in 2000 and, more recently, the United Nations Conference on Sustainable Development in 2012, thereby forming a basis for the 2030 Agenda for Sustainable Development.

Building on the linkages between population and environment, this developmental paradigm advocates an approach to development that integrates population dynamics. A number of perspectives have emerged to describe the best way for achieving this. Generally, the environmentalist perspective relates population growth to production and consumption patterns, and advocates a reduction in population growth in developing countries and a decrease in consumption patterns in developed countries. The population perspective, however, promotes the integration of all aspects of population dynamics into sustainable development and the 2030 Agenda for Sustainable Development, given that these dynamics have great implications for the sustainability of the natural resources and vice versa.

Given that both water scarcity and population dynamics cut through all three pillars of sustainable development,[2] this chapter defines the concept of vulnerability to water scarcity in the context of sustainable development. It highlights the impact of water scarcity on population issues, making a case for considering a population-centred approach when addressing water-scarcity issues. The chapter explains how exposure, which is a component of vulnerability, is linked to the environmental pillar of sustainable development. It further attempts to elaborate on a number of factors influencing resilience of specific units of concern, such as specific sociodemographic groups. It endeavours to elucidate the relationships linking the resilience element of vulnerability to the economic and social pillars of sustainable development, demonstrating that water scarcity has differentiated impacts on different population groups, and highlighting that the impact of water scarcity varies considerably according to such factors as age, gender and socioeconomic status.

The report reflects the three layers of analysis, namely: (a) the nexus of sustainable development and water scarcity; (b) groups located at the intersection of the nexus; and (c) specific groups within a particular context and geographic location. While chapter I describes the nexus, this chapter focuses in particular on specific population and sociodemographic groups, and chapter III looks at vulnerability and its components using situational analyses of specific groups in particular national settings. This chapter delves into the exposure and resilience components of vulnerability, with the issue of sensitivity added to the investigation in chapter III within the context of specific country situations. In other words, the analysis in this chapter provides an entry point to chapter III in which in-depth case studies are presented to scrutinize all three components of vulnerability.

## B. Defining vulnerability

The research on vulnerability is mostly linked to the coupled human-environment system, and has come up with numerous definitions.[3, 4] In the context of this report, vulnerability is defined as "the risk of adverse outcomes to receptors or exposure units (human groups, ecosystems, and communities) in the face of relevant changes in climate, other environmental variables and social conditions".[5]

Risk is defined as "the probability of harmful consequences or expected losses resulting from a given hazard to a given element at danger or peril over a specified time period".[6] Whereas risk, in its rudimentary conception, is about the likelihood of an event happening and the extent of the impact of that event, vulnerability has a more sophisticated understanding of impact that takes into consideration its causes and consequences, recognizing the differentiated impact on different exposure units.

Examining the consequences of vulnerability leads to considering different factors which place people at risk, such as vulnerability in terms of health, loss of life, food security, livelihoods and poverty, among others.

When such consequences are associated with the social sphere, the vulnerability becomes a social vulnerability. Economic vulnerability is associated with changes in economic indicators, while environmental vulnerability is related to the susceptibility of the environment to any potential impact. The use of the term "population vulnerability" is meant to highlight differentiated impact on population groups, aiming to advocate a population-centred approach to policy development.

The concept of vulnerability is based on the premise that human actors always react in the face of environmental threats, and their actions need to be analysed as independent variables not only as responses to the hazards they face.[7] Vulnerability is a multidimensional concept and is a function of three main elements: (a) sensitivity; (b) degree of exposure; and (c) resilience.[8]

For the purpose of this report, vulnerability is considered as a function of the exposure to hazards, and the sensitivity and resilience of the system experiencing the hazards put greater emphasis on non-natural factors. The differentiation between natural hazards and natural disasters has made it possible to go beyond geophysical events to incorporate human systems.[9] In other words, two units of concern may have different vulnerabilities to similar hazards that they face,[10] given that vulnerability is at the same time a function of the context (social, economic, political) as well as the type of hazard in question.[11] Vulnerability is an intrinsic characteristic of a community,[12] given that the vulnerability considered in this study is what may be referred to as social vulnerability.[13] Vulnerability reflects the interaction between the exposure and resilience of a place and social profile of communities.[14] Moreover, an "adequate theory of vulnerability must explain changes in the number, size, kinds and characteristics of social units at various levels of analysis".[15]

## 1. Exposure

When considering the exposure element of vulnerability, such terms as magnitude, duration and frequency of the stress are repeated in several studies and reports.[16] Exposure is thus mainly associated to the hazard itself and is "characterized by the focus on the distribution of some hazardous condition, the human occupancy of this hazardous zone and the degree of loss associated with the occurrence of a particular event".[17] The exposure element can therefore be linked to the environmental pillar of sustainable development. In the context of this report, the focus is on the exposure to water and the sociodemographic characteristics of the population impacted by the extent of their exposure.

## 2. Sensitivity

The definition of sensitivity proposed by the Intergovernmental Panel on Climate Change (IPCC) is "the degree to which an exposure unit is affected by or responsive to climate stimuli".[18] Within this framework, exposure includes "any set of stresses",[19] or "perturbations".[20] Sensitivity is closely linked to the geographic location and emerges as an element of vulnerability that combines both exposure and resilience. Consequently, vulnerability is a function of the biophysical risk alongside the social response that occurs in a specific geographic setting.[21] This element could be closely linked to the impact, whether direct or indirect, on a particular system and translated through context-specific determinants.[22] Accordingly, the sensitivity element is analysed in chapter III within the context of case studies that focus on specific situations within well-defined geographic locations. Given that the elements identified in any vulnerability assessment, particularly those aimed at advancing sustainability, emphasize the role of institutions operating as stressors or a structure affecting system sensitivity and resilience,[23] the case studies will specifically seek to understand the

relevant institutional contexts that influence the water supply and demand or any other institutional frameworks.

## 3. Resilience

Resilience is the element that distinguishes the concept of vulnerability from the concept of risk.[24] Specifically, while vulnerability is seen as a concept that combines the notions of risk and resilience, resilience is defined as "the capacity of a system, community or society potentially exposed to hazards to adapt by resisting or changing in order to reach and maintain an acceptable level of functioning and structure".[25] Resilience entails the learning capacity from past experiences of a social system for better long-term protection.[26] It presents a major difference when compared to coping capacity given that it encompasses both the ex-ante vulnerability of a system and its ex-post capacity to cope with damages that result from hazards. By contrast, coping capacity is associated with measures taken in the aftermath of an extreme event.[27] Resilience is therefore closely associated with the social construction of vulnerability as it is embedded in and conditioned by the historical, cultural, social and economic characteristics of societies.[28] This association directly leads to linking the resilience element of vulnerability to the social and economic pillars of sustainable development. The resilience element of vulnerability to water scarcity is predominantly associated with such factors as poverty, unemployment, inequality, health, education and gender.

## C. Factors impacting vulnerability

Achieving sustainable development and enhancing resilience to water scarcity will only be possible when accounting fully for population dynamics and understanding the specific factors that affect the capacity of various units of concern (specific population

## Box 2. Vulnerability in the context of sustainable development

(a) Environmental vulnerability

"Healthy, productive and protective environments, social systems and economies are the basis of sustainable development and human welfare. The environment is the source of all our raw materials and absorbs the pollution from our activities. In turn, whilst going about our daily business (social and economic) we use the environment and convert its resources and natural services into those that directly support us. The problem is that all of these systems can be damaged, overloaded, or prevented from meeting our needs. By our own choices we can to a large extent determine our own quality of life, the condition of our lands and opportunities for future generations.

Vulnerability is a new way of looking at an age-old problem. Instead of focusing just on what has been going wrong in the past and the effects of hazards, vulnerability gives us the opportunity to focus on warning signs and getting things right for the future. As a future-focused approach, vulnerability is a way of using strengths and strategically improving weaknesses".[a]

(b) Economic vulnerability

The Economic Vulnerability Index as used by the United Nations Committee for Development Policy, which is an advisory body to the United Nations Economic and Social Council, is one of the criteria in the identification of LDCs measuring the structural vulnerability of countries to exogenous economic and environmental shocks. The Index contains indicators, namely population size, remoteness, merchandise export concentration, share of agriculture, forestry and fisheries in the gross domestic product, share of population affected by natural factors, instability of agricultural production and of exports of goods and services, which are grouped into various subgroups. It measures the structural vulnerability of countries to exogenous economic and environmental shocks.

## Composition of the Economic Vulnerability Index (EVI)

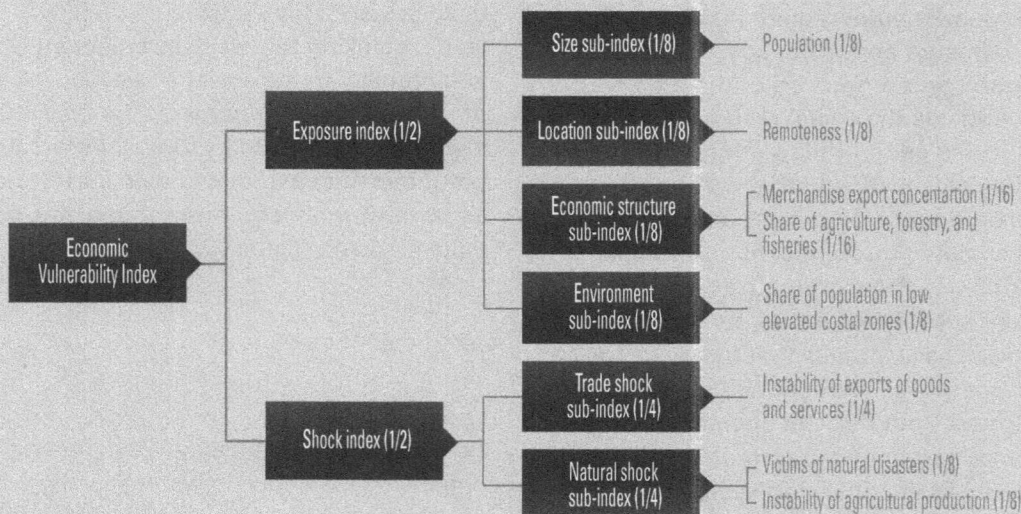

```
                                                    Size sub-index (1/8)  →  Population (1/8)

                          Exposure index (1/2)  →   Location sub-index (1/8)  →  Remoteness (1/8)

                                                    Economic structure         ┌ Merchandise export concentartion (1/16)
                                                    sub-index (1/8)  →          └ Share of agriculture, forestry, and
                                                                                  fisheries (1/16)
Economic
Vulnerability Index
                                                    Environment                Share of population in low
                                                    sub-index (1/8)  →          elevated costal zones (1/8)

                                                    Trade shock                Instability of exports of goods
                                                    sub-index (1/4)  →          and services (1/4)
                          Shock index (1/2)  →
                                                    Natural shock               ┌ Victims of natural disasters (1/8)
                                                    sub-index (1/4)  →          └ Instability of agricultural production (1/8)
```

Source: United Nations Economic and Social Council, Committee for Development Policy (CDP), 2015.
Note: Numbers in parenthesis indicate the weight in the overall EVI.

(c) Social vulnerability

"Social vulnerability is most often described using the individual characteristics of people (age, race, health, income, type of dwelling unit, employment). Social vulnerability is partially the product of social inequalities – those social factors that influence or shape the susceptibility of various groups to harm and that also govern their ability to respond. However, it also includes place inequalities – those characteristics of communities and the built environment, such as the level of urbanization, population growth, and economic vitality, that contribute to the social vulnerability of places. Socially created vulnerabilities are largely ignored, mainly owing to the difficulty in quantifying them, which also explains why social losses are normally absent in after-disaster cost/loss estimation reports."[b]

[a] Secretariat of the Pacific Community (SPC), Environmental Vulnerability Index. Available from www.sopac.org/environmental-vulnerability-index.
[b] S.L. Cutter, B.J. Boruff and W.L. Shirley, "Social vulnerability to environmental hazards", *Social Science Quarterly*, vol. 84, No. 2 (2003), pp. 242-261; and W.N. Adger, "Vulnerability", *Global Environmental Change*, vol. 16, No. 3 (2006), pp. 268-281.

groups, countries or individuals). Moreover, a failure to integrate fully and appropriately population dynamics into water management and sustainable development policies can further exacerbate the overall vulnerability of population groups and limit their ability to adapt to water stress. This, in turn, undermines the basic rights of these population groups and limits progress towards achieving the 2030 Agenda for Sustainable Development.

The causes of vulnerability can be linked to social, economic and political structures, and environmental settings.[29] The focus on the causes of vulnerability leads to an array of complex factors – interlinked and interdependent variables – that impact vulnerability in a non-linear fashion. Moreover, these causes of vulnerability are multidimensional (social, economic and such environmental factors as poverty and gender) and therefore any presentation of a comprehensive measurement framework to quantify exactly the impact of these forces would not be possible. However, it is possible to simulate real-life scenarios and offer some predictive capacity to conceptualize "what may happen" to a specific unit of concern under conditions of particular risk and hazards.[30]

As such, this chapter examines population vulnerability to demonstrate and highlight the differentiated impacts that the same stressor may have a different impact on various population subgroups or sociodemographic groups. Specifically, within the same sociodemographic group, such as farmers in a selected area, for example, a given stressor may have differentiated impacts on younger and older groups. It is therefore necessary to follow a population-centred approach that aims to reduce vulnerability of various population and sociodemographic groups.

Based on the linkages and relationships between water scarcity and population dynamics developed in chapter I, this chapter introduces factors related to the three pillars of sustainable development revolving around the individual components of vulnerability. To examine the exposure component of vulnerability, the environmental pillar of sustainable development and indicators related to water resources have to be considered. The examination of the resilience element relies on social and economic pillars of sustainable development, in particular those related to poverty, education, health and inequality. While the overview of factors, including political ones, does not identify all vulnerable groups to water scarcity in the region, it does offer an innovative, population-centred way of looking at and considering the issue of water scarcity. The analysis of these factors is complemented by examples of population and sociodemographic groups and the analysis of their exposure and adaptive capabilities in relation to water scarcity.

Given country heterogeneity, it is difficult to compile, in a systematic manner and at the national level, a defined set of indicators that can quantify the impact of various factors in particular settings. For instance, indicators related to the agricultural sector are much more relevant and important to Egypt than to the United Arab Emirates given the weight of the agricultural sector in Egypt in terms of employment and contribution to the gross domestic product (GDP). Rather than building an exhaustive list of indicators correlating to the three pillars of sustainable development, or a universal measurement framework for various national contexts, the analysis presented here provides a snapshot of groups selected in advance, including farmers, internally displaced and forced migrants and people living under the poverty line. This is broken down further by such factors as gender and age, thereby demonstrating the differential impact on these groups.

The impact of these factors can be studied on various units of concern, such as individuals, population groups or countries. A distinctly different analysis would be required to assess the resilience of an entire country to that of a population group or a set of individuals. Consideration of scale is also essential, as is conducting a proper analysis at each level. National vulnerability is not, in any case, a sum of the local vulnerabilities and a low vulnerability at a national level does not necessarily mean a low vulnerability at all levels. While an analysis at a national level could serve as an entry point for both understanding and addressing the processes that cause and exacerbate vulnerability, it is also essential to

consider the way in which the impact at such a level can be mediated by local conditions and vice versa.[31] As such, the terminology "population vulnerability" is used in this context to support the above argument and to advocate an approach that leads to identifying the impact on different units of concern (population or sociodemographic groups).

The extent to which water scarcity is distributed between people and ecosystems depends on the prevailing environmental, economic, social and political setting. The sections below investigate the impact of these factors.

## 1. Environmental factors

The Arab region receives 2.1 per cent of the global average annual precipitation and holds 1.2 per cent of the annual renewable freshwater resources of the world. Yet, it accounts for 10 per cent of the world's land mass and is home to more than 5 per cent of the world's total population.[32] The region is subject to low and variable precipitation, and is characterized by an arid and a semi-arid climate and high evaporation rates, diminishing the water remaining as surface run-off or groundwater recharge.[33]

In 2014, 18 Arab countries already faced severe water scarcity, with average water availability per capita below the water poverty line of 1,000 cubic metres per capita per year; and 13 countries were under the 500 cubic metres per year threshold set by the World Health Organization as a benchmark for severe scarcity. Even more, nine countries were below 200 cubic metres per capita per year (figure 7). It is estimated that by 2025, Iraq and Mauritania could be the only Arab countries with an average renewable water resource of 1,000 cubic metres per capita per year or above (figure 9).[34]

The region is highly reliant on surface waters, accounting for no less than 80 per cent

**Figure 7.** Total renewable water resources in Arab countries, 2014
(Cubic metres per capita per year)

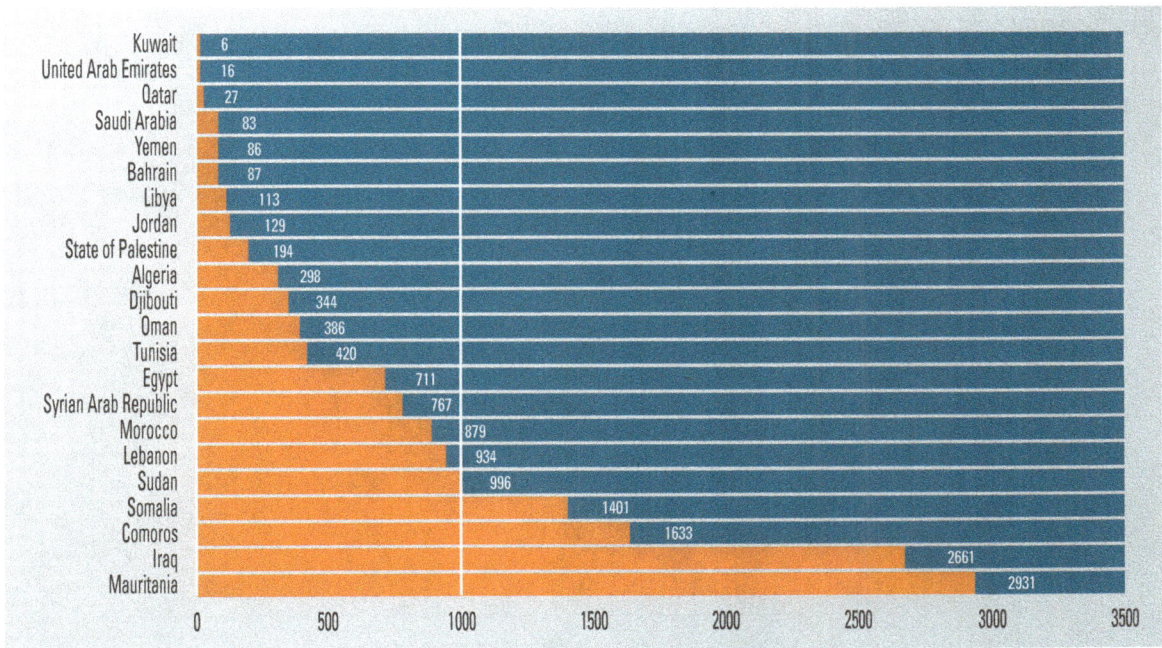

|  |  |
|---|---|
| Kuwait | 6 |
| United Arab Emirates | 16 |
| Qatar | 27 |
| Saudi Arabia | 83 |
| Yemen | 86 |
| Bahrain | 87 |
| Libya | 113 |
| Jordan | 129 |
| State of Palestine | 194 |
| Algeria | 298 |
| Djibouti | 344 |
| Oman | 386 |
| Tunisia | 420 |
| Egypt | 711 |
| Syrian Arab Republic | 767 |
| Morocco | 879 |
| Lebanon | 934 |
| Sudan | 996 |
| Somalia | 1401 |
| Comoros | 1633 |
| Iraq | 2661 |
| Mauritania | 2931 |

Source: FAO, Aquastat (2014). Available from www.fao.org/nr/water/aquastat/data/query/.

**Figure 8.** Total renewable water resources in Arab countries, 1982-2012
(Cubic metres per capita per year)

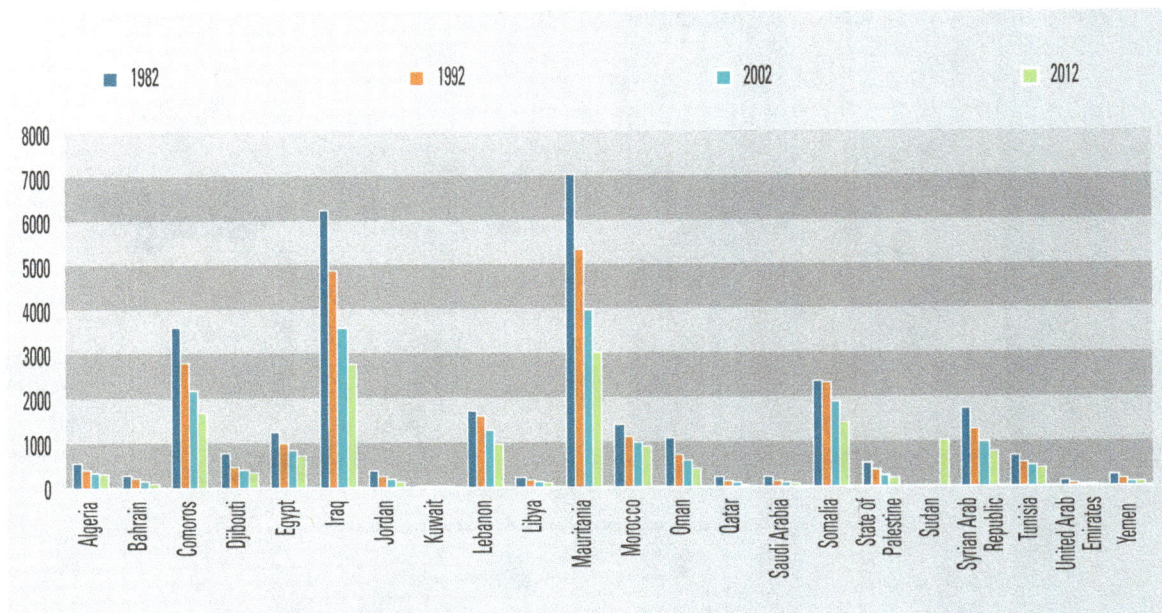

Legend: ■ 1982  ■ 1992  ■ 2002  ■ 2012

Source: FAO, Aquastat (2014). Available from www.fao.org/nr/water/aquastat/data/query/.

**Figure 9.** Projections of total renewable water resources in Arab countries, 2000, 2025 and 2050 (Cubic metres per capita per year)

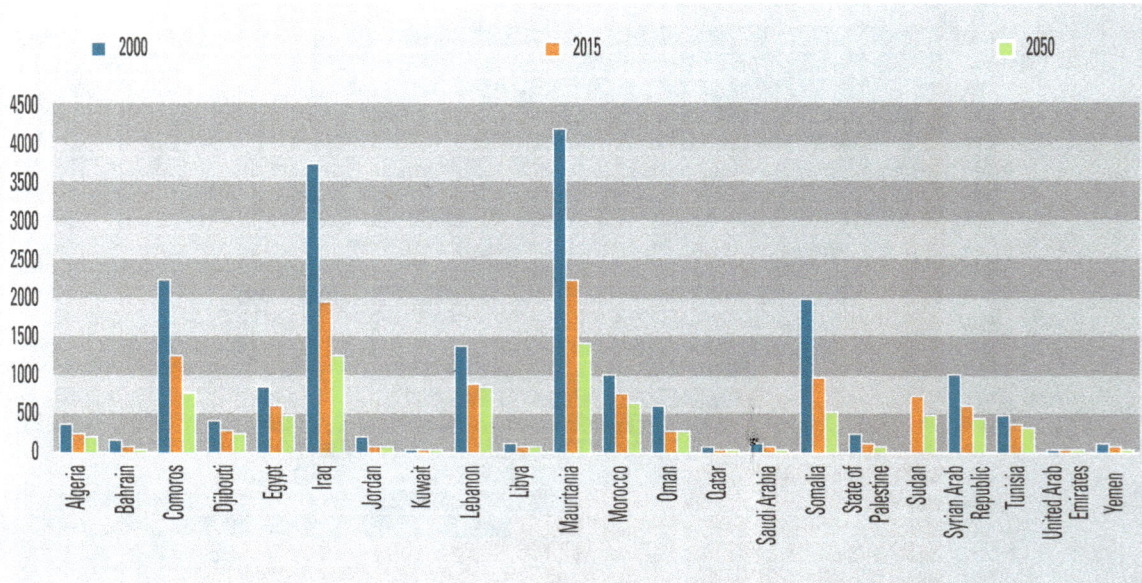

Source: FAO, Aquastat (2014). Available from www.fao.org/nr/water/aquastat/data/query/.

of total freshwater resources. The picture becomes more alarming when noting that over 60 per cent of surface water originates outside the region, mainly in Turkey and the Ethiopian Plateau.[35] In total, the Arab region comprises 23 main watersheds, including a few medium-sized rivers that originate and flow within the national boundaries of one country; major rivers originating from outside the region; and rivers shared by more than

**Map 1.** Water withdrawal as a percentage of total available water, 1995 and 2025

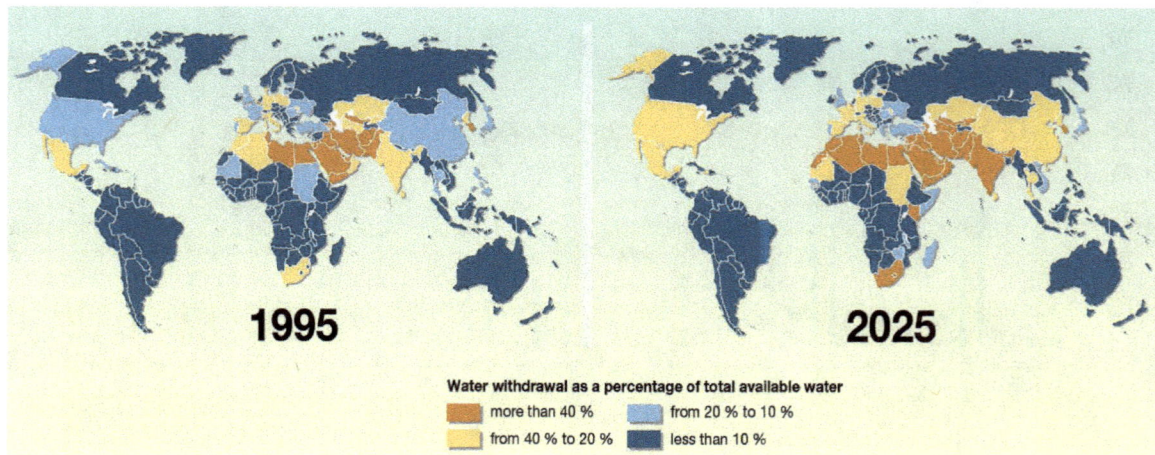

Source: UNEP, Vital Water Graphics: An Overview of the State of the World's Fresh and Marine Waters (2008). Available from www.unep.org/dewa/vitalwater/article141.html.

one Arab country, such as Jordan, Lebanon and the Syrian Arab Republic.[36] Groundwater resources are mainly recharged by rivers and by precipitation. In several such Arab countries as Bahrain, Jordan, Lebanon, Oman, Tunisia, United Arab Emirates and Yemen, more than 50 per cent of the total water withdrawals are from groundwater resources, reaching up to 84 per cent of all water withdrawal in certain Arab countries.[37] While water resources in the Arab region are limited, overexploitation of renewable and non-renewable groundwater resources and their use beyond their natural replenishment rates lead to the depletion of aquifer reserves (map 1). Pollution further reduces water supplies and therefore leads to the exacerbation of water scarcity. The region's chronic water scarcity is further exacerbated by the effects of climate change. The generated projections of precipitation during the summer months show that precipitation will exhibit large variability, with the change over the Arab region ranging from -0.5 to 0.5 mm/day with reduced patterns in precipitation towards the end of the century.[38] Rising temperatures in the Arab region will also lead to severe desiccation in the decades to come. While rising temperatures will certainly lead to greater evaporation and water losses, there is great uncertainty over the magnitude and direction of expected changes in rainfall.[39] Temperature increases are also likely to reduce the snow cover in the Euphrates and Tigris watersheds, which

would consequently reduce the discharge of the region's rivers and streams, particularly the Euphrates and Tigris rivers. Seawater intrusion owing to climate change can lead to salinization and the degradation of water quality.[40] Such developments can further affect negatively agriculture and food security and cause famine and malnutrition. The fluctuation in agriculture yields will increase and their stabilization will eventually occur at lower averages.[41]

## 2. Economic factors

Various economic factors have to be taken into consideration when describing vulnerability to water scarcity, including poverty, employment, income, industry and agricultural production. Conversely, water is a vital resource that influences human livelihoods and socioeconomic development. The relationship between water and poverty is described as being a vicious circle and an issue of life and of livelihoods.[42] Access to water constitutes a great challenge facing the poor, many of whom live in areas where the water and sanitation infrastructure is weak or not existent. The quality and quantity of supplied water are a greater health burden on poor populations, which further prevents them from overcoming poverty. Moreover, the poor usually set their livelihood – that is highly impacted by water scarcity – as a first priority, together with health and education.

**Box 3.** Vulnerability of the rural poor to water scarcity in Morocco

(a) Exposure to water scarcity

The population of Morocco, estimated at 33.9 million in 2015, is expected to reach approximately 42.9 million in 2050. The total fertility rate in Morocco has decreased from 5.40 children per woman in 1980-1985 to 2.38 children per woman in 2005-2010, and is projected to increase in 2010-2015 to 2.78 children per woman. The population growth rate is expected to decrease from the current 1.41 per cent to reach 0.3 per cent in 2045-2050. Yet, the absolute number of rural dwellers has been increasing from 11.5 million in 1980 and is expected to reach almost 14 million in 2015, applying pressure on already limited water resources and an underdeveloped water infrastructure in the rural areas of Morocco.[a]

The country is facing challenges with regard to providing access to water for its population, particularly given the decreasing per capita renewable water resources (from 1,134 cubic metres in 1992 to 878.6 cubic metres in 2014) and the increasing annual freshwater withdrawal as a proportion of the total renewable water resource (from 35.7 per cent in 2010 to 43.5 per cent in 2012). The proportion of agricultural water withdrawal as a percentage of total withdrawal was high, at 87.7 per cent, representing an increase from 74.5 per cent in 2002. This is particularly pertinent given that most of the agriculture is concentrated in rural areas, making the livelihoods of rural communities dependent on water.

## (b) Resilience to water scarcity

In 2013, GDP per capita stood at $3,146. The Moroccan economy consolidated its growth in 2013, with GDP rising by 4.7 per cent compared to 2.7 per cent in 2012, despite the slowdown in global economic growth. This is owed mostly to a vibrant agricultural sector.[b] Agricultural land covers almost 70 per cent of the total land area. Unemployment stood at 7.2 per cent, with youth unemployment above the national average at 9.4 per cent. The proportion of the population using improved drinking water sources was 87 per cent in 2012, with the rural population having slightly more limited access in comparison to urban population (73 per cent and 78 per cent, respectively). In total, 9 per cent of Morocco's population was living under the poverty line in 2007, the latest year for which data is available.[c] Rural poverty was much higher than the national average, with 14 per cent of rural population living in poverty, which represents more than 2 million poor concentrated in rural areas.[d] Some 75 per cent of rural poor people depend on agriculture for a livelihood.[e]

## (c) Rural population as specific sociodemographic group vulnerable to water scarcity

Morocco is a middle-income country with good water infrastructure that provides access to safe drinking water and sanitation to the majority of the urban population. Deteriorating infrastructure, however, affects the poor in rural settings; and extending water services to this group remains an ongoing challenge. Providing services to smaller communities by developing domestic water connections is costly and, possibly, a loss-making business. Integrated reading of indicators and soft intelligence suggests that the lack of adaptive capacity in relation to water scarcity is impacting such sectors as agriculture, which are fundamentally important to rural populations. Water is an important source of livelihood for 39 per cent of the population, representing the population engaged in agriculture, most of whom are in rural settings, including mountainous zones and semi-arid plains and uplands. Moreover, the proportion of the rural population with access to improved water sources is well below the national average of 84 per cent. This is pertinent, particularly given that a larger proportion of people below the poverty line are concentrated in rural settings, thereby making rural populations more vulnerable and less capable to adapt to water scarcity.[f]

[a] ESCWA, *The Demographic Profiles of the Arab Countries.*
[b] African Development Bank Group, "Morocco economic outlook". Available from www.afdb.org/en/countries/north-africa/morocco/morocco-economic-outlook/ (accessed 19 February 2015).
[c] The World Bank, Poverty headcount ratio at national poverty lines. Available from http://data.worldbank.org/indicator/SI.POV.NAHC/countries/MA?display=graph (accessed 19 February 2015).
[d] Rural Poverty Portal, Morocco statistics. Available from www.ruralpovertyportal.org/en/country/statistics/tags/morocco (accessed 19 February 2015).
[e] Rural Poverty Portal, "Rural poverty in the Kingdom of Morocco". Available from www.ruralpovertyportal.org/country/home/tags/morocco (accessed 19 February 2015).
[f] L. Achy, *Morocco's Experience with Poverty Reduction: Lessons for the Arab World* (Washington, D.C., Carnegie Endowment for International Peace, 2010). Available from http://carnegieendowment.org/files/morocco_poverty1.pdf.

Poor households, which tend to pay more for water, suffer the most from water scarcity, contamination and inadequate sanitation (box 3). A study by the United Nations Development Programme (UNDP) indicates that people living in slum areas in developing countries pay five to ten times more per water unit than those connected to piped water.[43]

The industry sector helps promote economic growth and is important for economic diversification and job creation. Nevertheless, increased industrial pollution and waste are harming ecosystems and jeopardizing water resources, thereby weakening water security for both people and industries that depend on water. Putting in place new or enhancing regulatory and institutional frameworks that promote good environmental and water governance will help control industrial water pollution, improve the productivity of the water used and, in effect, preserve water quantity and support sustainable economic growth. The water needs of the industrial sector are justified given that no manufacturing can take place without water. However, balancing such demands with those of other sectors is of utmost importance.

The energy sector also requires reliable, continuous and sustainable water supply. Energy and water are interdependent, given that water is needed to generate energy, and that energy is needed to generate and deliver freshwaters supplies. In principle, energy-intensive water delivery systems, including thermal desalination and water pumping, can have severe consequences in regions that are water and energy scarce. At the same time, ensuring efficient energy use in water and wastewater industries brings down the costs of maintenance, operation and supply, reduces emissions and enhances, among other things, the quality of water and service coverage. This can be made possible by upgrading the design and operation of energy delivery systems.

Globally, the agriculture sector has so far fared well in meeting the challenge of coping with ever-rising populations by increasing per capita food production. The sector is mostly rain-fed, with irrigation used to supplement rainfall. This is particularly important in areas that are vulnerable to excessive climatic variability in order to ensure the necessary water supply for crop production. Irrigation is one of the largest consumers of water resources. Agriculture is the biggest water consumer, with the share of agricultural water withdrawal exceeding 90 per cent in such countries as Mauritania, Somalia, the Sudan and Yemen.[44] Considering that agriculture consumes the bulk of water resources, the future challenge will be to ensure that resources used in this sector are used more efficiently (for example, through drip irrigation) so that even more food can be produced with less water. This would, in effect, make scarce water resources available for both household consumption and more productive uses in industry, as well as services and hydropower.

Examples from the region show that agricultural areas that rely mainly on rainfall for water are extremely impacted by drought, with farmers being mostly affected. Such droughts result in decreasing yields, negatively influencing the ability of farmers to meet their food needs, and thereby rendering them food insecure and causing them to resort to such harmful practices as reducing their food intake. Droughts also deplete vegetation in pasture lands, forcing farmers to sell their livestock, sometimes even below cost, to avoid a total loss resulting from the death of herds. Selling the livestock, which is a livelihood asset for famers, is also induced by the lack of income and the inability to meet basic necessities.[45] This situation further increases the vulnerability of farmers and their households, with the threat of falling into poverty. Desertification is another consequence brought about by droughts, jeopardizing biodiversity, threatening the survival abilities of human communities, and decreasing the areas covered by native plants which signals land degradation.[46]

As noted above, the shortage of rainfall water and subsequent droughts threaten rain-fed agriculture, which can result in significant pressure on economic and social stability in countries that depend heavily on agriculture. Besides, water scarcity causes competition for water between different sectors, beneficiaries and consumers. Conflicts over water between communities at the local level can arise in water-stressed areas owing to the fact that sharing such a scarce and vital resource is highly challenging. The impact of water shortage and droughts can also lead to possible tension and conflict between countries, particularly when they depend on shared water resources, such as transboundary rivers and flows. There is a need to devise and enforce adequate legal instruments in order to ensure a fair and equitable allocation of water resources and prevent chaos and friction between different competing parties.[47]

## 3. Social factors

Human capital development, education and health affect resilience to water scarcity. Conversely, human health is highly affected by the availability and quality of water, which has a bearing on sanitation and hygiene policies that support human capital formation.[48] Consequently, poverty, poor health and education are considered as determinants of vulnerability to water scarcity as they reduce or enhance the resilience of exposed populations. These determinants are likely to impact vulnerability to various hazards and in different locations and contexts.[49] An extensive body of literature shows the complex and entangled relationships linking poverty, health, employment and inequality.[50] Some literature is more focused on resilience to environmental stress, arguing that education is a parameter that enhances the resilience of the population to natural disasters.[51] Essentially, the consequences ensuing from water scarcity, such as famine and migration, vary according to the social standing of people and are "rather part of an overall livelihood situation that involves opportunities and constraints that delimit feasible coping strategies".[52]

Different social groups, such as youth, older persons or women, differ in their capabilities to overcome their vulnerability to water scarcity.

Paying special attention to the empowerment and inclusion of marginalized groups enhances their resilience.[53] For example, seizing the benefits that could come with population ageing requires promoting active and healthy ageing.[54] Concentrated efforts will be needed to tackle the concerns of older groups and the realization of their developmental potential. In addition to investing in social protection systems, including pension schemes, health systems need to shift their focus from communicable to non-communicable diseases that come with ageing.[55] Moreover, providing lifelong education and combating discrimination are important facets of this strategy.[56]

Women represent another group that is disadvantaged in many aspects of social and economic life, which can in effect impact on their capacity to cope with water scarcity (box 4). According to the World Bank, female labour force participation for the Arab region was estimated at 23 per cent in 2013. This figure might be overestimated given that labour force participation rates in the Gulf subregion reflect the high number of foreign female domestic workers.[57] Consequently, less than one-quarter of the labour force of the Arab region is made up of women; and the same population group accounts for almost 40 per cent of the unemployed population. In total, 70 to 80 per cent of women belonging to the working age in the Arab region are either inactive or unemployed.[58] Involvement in environmental decision-making remains weak, while women often bear the overall responsibility for water within households.

Policies directly addressing water scarcity need to be "rights based and gender responsive".[59] Women in the region are more likely to manage the household and, in effect, control water consumption, so they need to be targeted to raise awareness of water consumption. Access to safe water also plays an important part given that women are primary caretakers of family and children and require access to safe water

## Box 4. Vulnerability to water scarcity of small farmers in the Nile Delta and Valley, Egypt

The population of Egypt, which has grown from 72 million in 2006 to 88 million in 2015, is putting increasing pressures on the gradually limited national water resources. These increasing pressures affect groups of society differently; for instance, they have a sharp adverse impact on agricultural communities which depend on increasingly scarce water resources to maintain their agricultural livelihoods, particularly in newly reclaimed lands.

The reclamation of desert land in Egypt is motivated by government policies aimed at expanding agricultural production and at creating jobs for farming communities and, ultimately, at combating Egypt's hyperarid desert topography. Currently, reclaimed agricultural land is estimated to comprise up to 25 per cent of total agricultural lands nationwide.[a] These growing tracts of reclaimed land are complemented with targeted investments aimed at improving agricultural yields and efficiency in resource management, resulting in cereal yields per hectare that are comparable to the highest yields globally.

The Al-Minya Governorate in Upper Egypt is one area that attracts particular attention in terms of land reclamation. The Governorate is served by the man-made Ibrahimya canal which channels water from the Nile to irrigate more than half a million hectares of reclaimed land. The government recently announced new plans to accommodate 500,000 people and create 100,000 jobs in agriculture in the Western Desert plains of Al-Minya.[b]

However, this growth in land reclamation brings with it a number of hardships experienced by agricultural communities living and working in these reclaimed lands, including persistent poverty; variable and higher costs of irrigation and water; inadequate infrastructure; and limitations in the quality, availability and accessibility of social services. For instance, the population living below the poverty line in Al-Minya doubled from 15.1 per cent of the total Governorate population to 30.9 per cent between 2003 and 2009.[c] This can be associated with population growth in the Governorate, which increased from 4.1 million in 2006 to 5 million in 2015.

Rural agricultural communities, residing on both prime and reclaimed lands are generally characterized by a large family size and high fertility rates. Moreover, they typically face a wide range of economic and social challenges, such as child labour, poverty and lack of access to basic social services. Furthermore, while these new reclaimed lands provide new opportunities, these same opportunities are not ecologically – and thus economically – sustainable owing to the foreseeable shortages in access to needed water resources.[d] An empirical study that compared the nature of the challenges faced in two agricultural communities in Al-Minya, one on prime land and the other on reclaimed lands, highlighted stark vulnerabilities around the latter's communities.[e] The study concluded that, although these new communities had a significantly higher understanding of the challenges associated with climate change and limited access to water, they were unable to cope with these challenges owing to significant resource and infrastructure limitations. The same study cited that 76 per cent of respondents in the reclaimed lands reported localized confrontations over irrigation water, compared to 40 per cent among respondents in prime agricultural lands.

### Women farmers in Al-Bahirah

Over 70 per cent of the population in the Al-Bahirah Governorate in Egypt's Nile Delta are within the working-age group (aged 15-64). Notwithstanding this favourable percentage, the population faces a number of underdevelopment challenges that curb their productivity, such as an illiteracy rate of 41.1 per cent, and a school non-enrolment rate between 6 and 10 per cent. Considering these factors, the high outward migration rate, at 3.4 per cent in 2014,[f] illustrates a critical concern regarding the number, nature and quality of development and productivity opportunities available for the people in Al-Bahirah.

One particular subgroup is young people in underserved agricultural communities across the Governorate. Reports indicate that the general dissatisfaction of young people, particularly young men, with the nature of agricultural-based opportunities creates a strong push factor for emigration through any means possible.[g] Generally, these young men show interest in employment opportunities that are not readily available in their local communities, including working in construction, industry, carpentry, plumbing, plastering and domestic trade.

This dynamic creates a change in gender roles, forcing rural women to take on the additional work burden in the agricultural sector in addition to their reproductive, household and community roles. For instance, 32 per cent of rural women in Al-Bahirah reported such additional burdens associated with securing sufficient water resources.[h] Another example is the tendency to avoid crop gleaning or cultivating crops that are more demanding physically, which effectively abolishes rotation among different crops in an agricultural cycle and results in degrading soil quality. These changes have critical long-term consequences over the viability of returns to agricultural activity and national food security objectives, which creates a vicious cycle of vulnerability and underdevelopment.

In conclusion, the two examples of Al-Minya and Al-Bahirah illustrate the particular vulnerabilities of two sociodemographic groups in Egypt to the declining access to sufficient water resources for agricultural activity. New farming communities in reclaimed lands continue to face increasing hardships associated with access to water, while women farmers in underserved rural communities in Al-Bahirah are forced to bear additional work responsibilities.

[a] a AUB, "Impact of population growth", p. 12.
[b] b Al-Wafd, "The launch of the reclamation of 4 million acres in the western plains of Al-Minya" (in Arabic), 15 May 2015.
[c] c Data from the Central Agency for Public Mobilization and Statistics (CAPMAS) in Egypt.
[d] d H.K. Adriansen, "Land reclamation in Egypt: A study of life in the new lands", *Geoforum*, vol. 40, No. 4 (2009), pp. 664-674.
[e] e M.S. Abdelwahab, "A comparative study of the rural family living adaptation within the framework of climate change in a newly reclaimed community and a traditional community in Minya governorate" (in Arabic), *Mansoura Journal of Agricultural Economics and Social Sciences*, vol. 2, No. 10 (2011), pp. 1399-1412.
[f] f Data from the Central Agency for Public Mobilization and Statistics in Egypt.
[g] g Heba Handoussa. UN report 2010. Situation Analysis: Key Development Challenges Facing Egypt 2010: 1-118.
[h] h Abdelwahab, "A comparative study of the rural family living adaptation within the framework of climate change in Minya and Bahirah governorates" (in Arabic), *Mansoura Journal of Agricultural Economics and Social Sciences*, vol. 2, No. 5 (2011).

and sanitation facilities. Moreover, policies protecting the reproductive health and rights of women to avoid unintended pregnancies, fight gender-based violence and child marriage, and address the unmet needs for family planning will have an effect on water resources. In effect, the availability of water resources can be improved through advancing the well-being of the population by reducing child and maternal morbidity and mortality, and the occurrence of unintended pregnancies, thereby contributing to lowering fertility rates and slowing down population growth.[60]

## 4. Political factors

The economic and social issues that perpetuate inequality and poverty in Arab societies are further exacerbated by a number of important geopolitical and security dynamics, violence and conflict. These can lead in turn to forced displacement and large-scale population movements, governance failures and instability which in effect make populations more vulnerable to water scarcity. Communities and countries struggle to meet the needs of displaced migrants that usually result in sudden and extreme increases in demand on water resources (box 5).

The effects of instability often hurt the business environment, resulting in disinvestment, increasing production costs, and deteriorations in labour market conditions ending in economic contraction. It is estimated that the GDP loss in the Syrian Arab Republic reached 16.7 per cent in 2013,[61] and 5.2 per cent in Libya in 2014.[62] Moreover, conflicts can lead to internal displacement of populations and refugee flows. For example, the conflict in the Syrian Arab Republic has so far directly affected around 12.2 million persons who have fled within or outside the national borders, with severe consequences on the well-being of people in the country, as

well as Syrian refugees and host communities in Egypt, Iraq, Jordan and Lebanon.

Many of the State-supported water management systems are not properly equipped in the institutional and technical sense to cope with water-scarcity challenges. This requires targeted investments aimed at modernizing and upgrading infrastructure in order to achieve gains in water productivity, reducing water losses and restructuring institutions to enhance a reliable water supply, equitable access and transparent management. Enhancing the management of water resources helps to stabilize agricultural production and increase productivity, thereby improving the livelihoods of rural populations and reducing their vulnerability. Conversely, conflict and civil unrest impede reforms and can lead to a deterioration of governance and management systems.

**Box 5.** Internally displaced populations and forced migrants as a specific sociodemographic group vulnerable to water scarcity in the Sudan

(a) Exposure to water scarcity

The population of the Sudan reached 39.6 million in 2015, and it is expected to almost double by 2050. Population growth rate is projected to rise to 2.33 per cent for the period 2015-2020 before decreasing gradually. The percentage of urban dwellers increased from 20 per cent in 1980 to 33.8 per cent in 2010. Population projections show that this percentage will continue to increase; and it is estimated that half of the Sudan's population will be living in urban settings by 2050 as a result of internal urban-rural migration.[a]

Population movements and international migration are important population factors in the Sudan. In addition to indigenous nomadic populations who make up 9 per cent of the population,[b] there were almost 450,000 international migrants in 2013. Irregular migrants also transit through the Sudan on their way to Libya, Egypt and other destinations.[c] Following the partition of the country and the independence of South Sudan, the number of internally displaced has been increasing. As of January 2015, there were up to 3.1 million IDPs in the Sudan, particularly in the region of Darfur and the states of South Kordofan and Blue Nile.[d]

(b) Resilience to water scarcity at the national level

The Sudan has suffered from various internal conflicts which started with a war in the south and lasted for more than 50 years. Consequently, the economic and social process has been affected by political instability and economic uncertainty which continue to determine wider social and economic outcomes for the population of the country. The economy remains largely dependent on oil and agriculture (with agricultural land covering 45.7 per cent of the country's landmass). A look at social, economic and water indicators suggests that, despite relatively high total renewable water per capita (995 m$^3$/per capita/per year in 2014), the overall resilience to water scarcity of some population groups is low. GDP per capita was one of the lowest in the region, at $1,753 in 2013, and nearly half of the population (46.6 per cent) lives in poverty. The highest incidence of poverty was recorded in North Darfur and the highest income inequality in Darfur and Kordofan, where the biggest concentration of forced migrants can be found, thereby making poverty eradication more challenging in these areas.[e] Only about 55 per cent of households in the Sudan have access to improved drinking water sources, while many Sudanese still rely on rivers, lakes, ponds and wells owing to the absence of piped drinking water.

## (c) Internally displaced populations and forced migrants

The Sudan is a country with limited water resources which has to respond to the additional burden of supplying water and sanitation to populations of international migrants, forced migrants, refugees and IDPs within its borders. Refugees are often left with inadequate shelter and sanitation facilities and a deficient amount of clean water. Rising floodwater is worsening the crisis. In 2013, at least 319,700 people were internally displaced as a result of flooding in 15 states, exceeding the total of 238,000 for the period 2008-2012. Water and sanitation assistance are crucial in emergencies. Yet, precarious situations leave migrants with limited access to improved water sources, suggesting that these populations are most at risk. Access to safe drinking water, sanitation and the promotion of hygienic practices are important factors for reducing the incidence of infectious diseases and preventing their transmission. For instance, diarrhoea and other gastrointestinal infections as well as various infectious diseases of the skin and eyes are connected with an inadequate supply of safe drinking water, hygiene and sanitation.[f] This is evident in refugee camps worldwide, where the occurrence of infectious diseases can be largely attributed to water shortages.[g] The complexity of challenges arising from protracted displacement put additional pressure on these communities in their ability to access water.

[a] ESCWA, *The Demographic Profiles of the Arab Countries.*
[b] UNFPA, Population Dynamics of Sudan. Available from countryoffice.unfpa.org/filemanager/files/sudan/facts/population_fact_sheet_final1.pdf.
[c] Ibid.
[d] Internal Displacement Monitoring Centre (IDMC), Global figures. Available from www.internal-displacement.org/global-figures#conflict (accessed 19 February 2015).
[e] United Nations in Sudan (n.d.), MDG 1: Eradicate Extreme Hunger and Poverty. Available from www.undp.org/content/unct/sudan/en/home/mdgs/overview/mdg1.html.
[f] United Nations Educational, Scientific and Cultural Organization (UNESCO), *World Water Development Report II - Water: A Shared Responsibility* (Paris, UNESCO, 2006).
[g] Dow and others, *Linking Water Scarcity*, p. 12.

# III. Case Studies

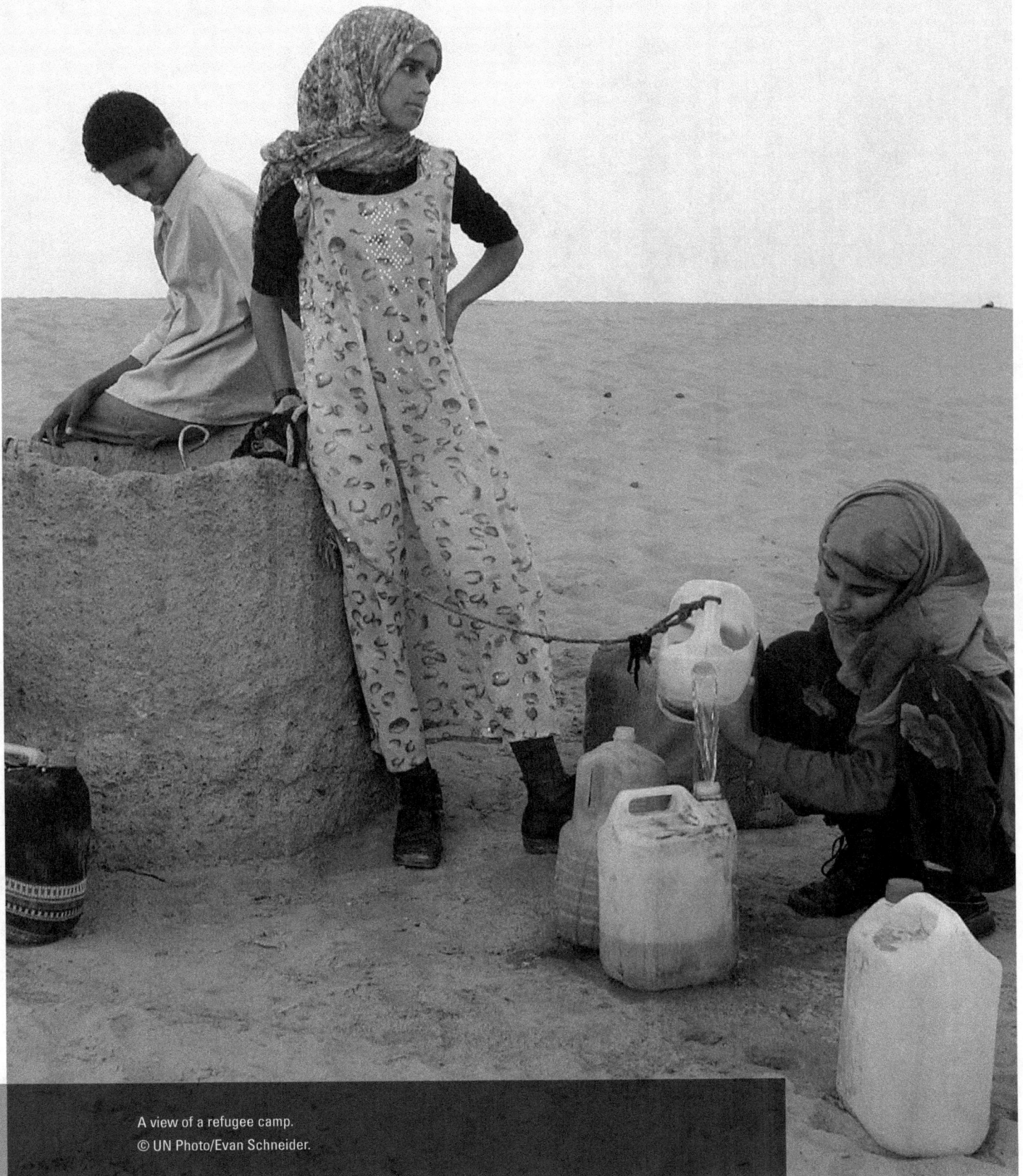

A view of a refugee camp.
© UN Photo/Evan Schneider.

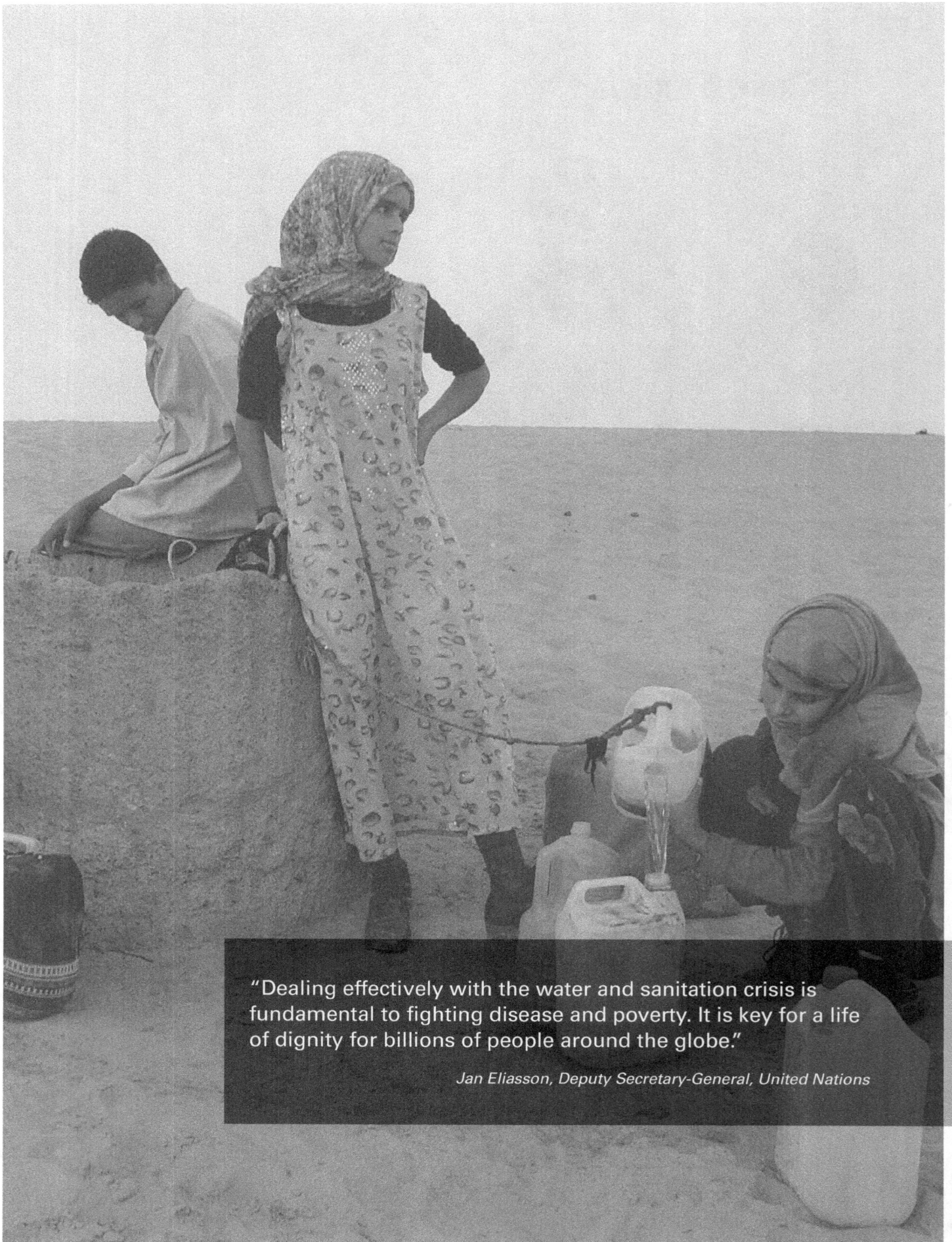

"Dealing effectively with the water and sanitation crisis is fundamental to fighting disease and poverty. It is key for a life of dignity for billions of people around the globe."

Jan Eliasson, Deputy Secretary-General, United Nations

# III. Case Studies

This chapter zooms in on specific vulnerable sociodemographic and population groups living in particular geographical locations. It provides context-specific analyses of exposure, sensitivity and resilience of specified population groups to overcome vulnerability to water scarcity.

The importance of spatial analysis has been extensively described in the literature given that "vulnerability rests in multifaceted coupled systems with connections operating at different spatio-temporal scales and commonly involving stochastic and nonlinear processes".[1] Furthermore, resilience is closely linked to local processes and measures,[2] and depends on vulnerability at the local level.[3] The case studies endeavour to compare exposure to water scarcity and resilience developed at the local level and to identify sensitivity (as defined in chapter II), which is closely linked to both the characteristics of sociodemographic groups and to geographic location. Given that assessing vulnerability entails a predictive quality that consists of conceptualizing "what may happen" to a specific unit of concern under conditions of particular risk and hazards,[4] the analysis aims to estimate the impact on vulnerable population groups in a context of scarce water resources, based on identifying mechanisms and measures that have already been put in place by local populations in different target areas.

The differentiated impact of water scarcity can be observed on various population and sociodemographic groups. For example, water scarcity that results in crop failure could affect women and men differently. Women losing their means of subsistence could be compelled to sell off such assets as livestock to respond to the needs of their families. By contrast, when losing their income streams, men might resort to migrating to other areas to seek alternative job opportunities. The impact on children could be entirely different. As school fees become unaffordable with a decreasing family income, children could be driven to drop out of school in order to support their families. A solid understanding of the roles that different users might have in ensuring access to or using water is crucial, as it allows identifying and implementing measures to reduce their vulnerability to water scarcity.

The three sites for the case studies, namely Sanaa in Yemen, and Mafraq and Jordan Valley in Jordan, were selected to focus on three sociodemographic groups that are particularly vulnerable to water scarcity: rural farmers, urban residents of informal settlements and migrants. The first case study tackles the urban population in Sana'a in Yemen, where water scarcity is mainly linked to physical scarcity and governance of the water sector. The second and third case studies concentrate on Jordan and compare the impact of water scarcity on the populations of two geographic areas, namely small and landless farmers in the Jordan Valley, and the urban population in Mafraq. The Jordan Valley case highlights the differentiated impact on landless farmers and women in rural areas as water scarcity leads to decreasing incomes, exacerbating poverty and challenges for women in terms of work load. Exposure to water scarcity in Mafraq is mainly linked to significant population growth, resulting from the influx of Syrian refugees coupled with a considerable physical water scarcity.

## A. Rural-urban migrants in Sana'a, Yemen

### 1. Introduction

Yemen, located on the southern coast of
the Arabian Peninsula, is one of the poorest
countries in the world. The climate is harsh
and the population of more than 25 million
people faces great challenges in the light
of rapidly declining water resources. The
political economy of water in Yemen – defined
by entwined economic realities, geopolitical
developments, migration and social
hierarchies – reflects the challenges
of sustainable development in a country
facing extreme water scarcity. Yemen is
experiencing a politically and economically
tumultuous period, with both the public
and private sectors having failed to address
food, water and energy insecurities facing
the country. The goal of this case study is to
understand the processes that have led to
water scarcity in Yemen and, specifically, in
its capital, Sana'a. Population vulnerability
to water scarcity is being examined and
identified, and particular focus is placed
on the urban poor and those living in
informal settlements within the city's
peripheries.

The opening of Yemen's markets to
international trade had a disastrous effect
on subsistence farmers. Specifically, local
producers could not compete with the cost
and quality of subsidized food imports,
which had the effect of dissuading local
subsistence farmers from producing the
crops needed for their survival. Similarly,
without local production of staple foods,
consumers came to be at the mercy of
fluctuating prices in the international market.
This is particularly relevant to a largely
impoverished national population. The
combination of these policies, with declining
water resources and uncoordinated national
conservation strategies, has set the stage
for widespread food insecurity. A report
by the World Food Programme estimated
that 56 per cent of the national population
experienced moderate to severe food
insecurity in 2012 (map 2).[5]

While the excessive and unregulated
production and marketing of qat is cause
for concern, the current crisis of Yemen's
agricultural industry can be attributed to
decades of development policies that have
undermined the local subsistence agro-
economy. Attributing failures in the sector
to individual farmers and their "traditional"
and "outdated" practices was first purported
in a 1979 World Bank report. It proposed that
farmers needed to adopt Western "modern"
agricultural techniques and to embrace
free-trade principles that opened markets
to transnational competition in order to
eradicate impoverishment. That strategy
simply missed the mark and these policies
have been nothing but a failure.[6]

The lack of effective policies has also been
aggravated by a politically weak Government
that has not found its footing since the
uprising in 2011. Political instability has its
roots in decades of internal political tensions
and armed conflict between warring factions,
as well as years of military interventions on
Yemen's territory.[7] The Government's inability
to address these broader national challenges
is paralleled by its inability to advocate
effective development policies, including
proper management of natural resources
and the provision of public goods and
services to marginalized populations.

### 2. Population indicators

These national developments have affected
more than 23 million Yemenis, a majority
of whom are under the age of 20.[8] While
the majority of the population lives in rural
areas, an urbanization rate of 4.8 per cent
has caused the population residing in
urban areas to swell from 22 per cent in
1990 to 33 per cent of the total population
in 2012.[9]

**Map 2.** Proportion of Yemeni households experiencing food insecurity by governorate

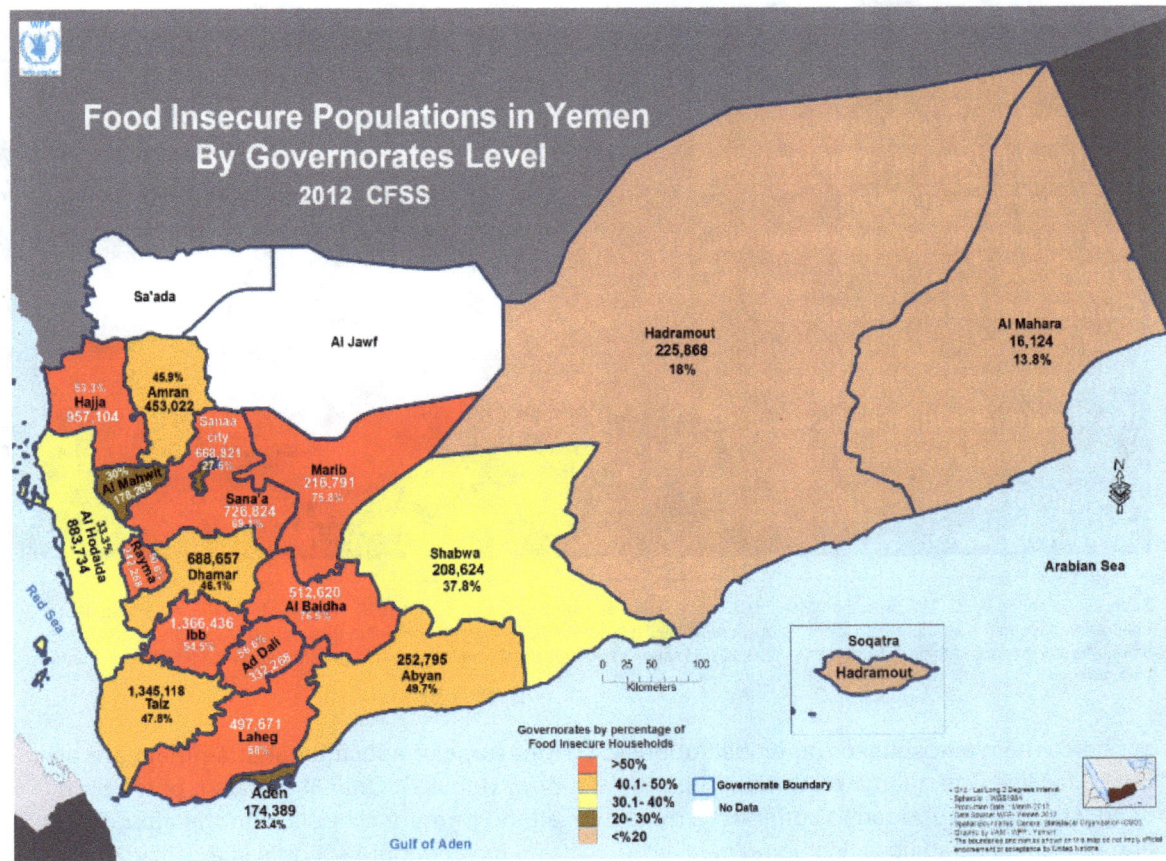

**Source:** World Food Programme (WFP), *The State of Food Security and Nutrition in Yemen: Summary and Overview. Comprehensive Food Security Survey* (Sana'a, 2012), p. 9. Available from https://www.wfp.org/content/yemen-comprehensive-food-security-survey-2012.

Yemen, which is already a resource-poor country, has an added population burden of roughly 500,000 migrants and refugees, the majority of whom have come from Somalia and the Horn of Africa in search of better economic opportunities and to escape violent conflict in their countries of origin.[10] These realities on the ground have led to a highly mobile population that relocates in response to land disputes, water shortages and civil unrest.[11] As of December 2014, UNHCR had registered 334,096 IDPs, and this number is constantly fluctuating.[12] Water scarcity is a common reason for displacement. For example, when a village runs out of water, residents seek alternative water sources elsewhere, either staying with nearby relatives or moving to urban areas. The length of their migration may be short term or prolonged, depending on the severity of the shortage. There are similar patterns of displacement and return during periods of armed conflict. Displaced Yemenis will often return to their land once violence ceases. Water-related displacement and armed conflict over scarce water resources may become more frequent and severe owing to the environmental pressures brought on by climate change.[13]

Yemen's demographic indicators are among the worst in the region, with the worst under-five and infant mortality rate in the region (table 1).[14] Moreover, only 36 per cent of births are attended by a skilled professional, and only 24 per cent

**Table 1.** Health and well-being indicators in Yemen

| | | Notes |
|---|---|---|
| Life expectancy at birth for men | 62 | 2012 |
| Life expectancy at birth for women | 65 | 2012 |
| Infant mortality rate (per 1,000 live births) | 69 | For five-year period preceding 2006 survey |
| Infants underweight at birth | 8 per cent | Last two years preceding survey |
| Maternal mortality ratio (per 100,000 live births) | 270 | 2013 |
| Children aged 2-9 with at least one disability | 25 per cent | 2006 |
| Use of improved drinking water sources | 59 per cent | 2006 |
| Use of improved sanitation facilities | 52 per cent | 2006 |
| Skilled attendant at delivery | 36 per cent | Last two years preceding survey |
| Institutional delivery | 24 per cent | 2005-2006 |
| Total fertility rate | 5.2 | Last three years preceding survey |

**Sources:** Compiled by ESCWA, based on Ministry of Health and Population in Yemen and UNICEF, "Yemen: Monitoring the situation of children and women – Multiple Indicator Cluster Survey 2006" (2008); WHO, 2012, Regional Health Observatory. Available from http://rho.emro.who.int/rhodata/?theme=country; and WHO, 2015, Yemen: WHO statistical profile. Available from http://www.who.int/gho/countries/yem.pdf?ua=1.

are held within a hospital or other institutional health facility. One quarter of Yemeni children aged 2 to 9 were reported to suffer from motor and/or mental disabilities, including delayed movements and an inability to understand instructions and to be understood.

Measures of educational attainment are also poor (table 2). Only 68 per cent of children attend primary schools, and the attendance rate in secondary schools is a paltry 24 per cent.[15] Low school attendance rates are mirrored by other data on the under-18

**Table 2.** Child education and labour statistics in Yemen, 2006 (Percentage)

| | |
|---|---|
| Pre-school attendance | 3 |
| Net intake rate in basic education | 40 |
| Net primary school attendance rate | 68 |
| Net secondary school attendance rate | 24 |
| Primary completion rate | 18 |
| Marriage before age 15 | 14 |
| Marriage before age 18 | 52 |
| Child labour | 23 |
| Adult literacy rate | 35 |

**Source:** Compiled by ESCWA, based on Ministry of Health and Population in Yemen and UNICEF, "Yemen: Monitoring the situation of children and women – Multiple Indicator Cluster Survey 2006" (2008).

population: 23 per cent of children engage in full- or part-time labour, while 14 per cent of children under the age of 15 are married and 52 per cent of children aged under 18 are married. Poor educational outcomes appear intergenerational, with adult-literacy rates reportedly as low as 35 per cent.

Around 42 per cent of the national population lives below the poverty line, with greater poverty in rural areas. In total, 21 per cent of urban households live in poverty, with 75 per cent of impoverished urban households concentrated in the cities of Sana'a and Aden.[16] While these numbers are substantial, they are probably underestimations of current conditions, which are expected to have deteriorated given the political climate and bombing campaigns across the country.

## 3. Water scarcity in Yemen

Various population groups are vulnerable to water scarcity across Yemen. Over the past 20 years, the country has witnessed diminishing availability of water, an increasing number of land and water disputes, transformation of the agricultural sector and persistent unregulated drilling of wells at a staggering pace.[17] There is growing public awareness of the water crisis. What began as a threat has turned into a dire reality over the years to the point where only 55 per cent of the population has access to improved water sources.[18] Successive Governments have not built the necessary infrastructure to regulate water extraction, which is occurring at an annual deficit of nearly 1.4 billion cubic metres. Table 3 shows changes to water and sanitation access and services for the urban and rural population since the unification of the country. The access to improved water sources varies significantly by region: in urban areas, 72 per cent of the population has access to improved water sources, compared to 47 per cent in rural areas.[19] Nationally, 59 per cent of households use

improved drinking water sources and 52 per cent have improved sanitation facilities. Three out of every ten households had water piped onto the premises.[20]

Yemen has a long history of engineering water management systems. Indeed, without this management of water resources, the country would not have succeeded in growing the rare crops for which it became famous at the height of its trade. Ward sums this history well: "It was water management, more than water resources endowment that earned Yemen the name 'Blessed Arabia'".[21] These practices remained relatively unchanged even up until the 1960s. There have been four distinctive stages of the water management policies since the unification of Yemen: first, the issue of water scarcity was largely ignored; next, the water scarcity threat and management oriented towards water demand became common knowledge; the third stage was characterized by institutional struggles over water management; and the latest and current stage is best categorized as a hiatus since the national water conference of 2011 and the fall of the Saleh regime.[22]

Prior to unification, water was regulated solely by the Government in the south; and in the former People's Republic of Yemen, drilling for water was undertaken by the private sector. Since the 1990s, there has been no clear strategy for regulating water extraction; rather, a laissez-faire approach has prevailed. The Government and international development agencies began to address the country's dwindling water supply only once it became a nationally recognized issue (box 6). However, by the time of their intervention in the 2000s, the agricultural lobby and tribal leaders had become powerful and resistant to demands for reform. Unfortunately, the prevailing approach has been largely limited to requesting the population to adapt to this dire reality.[23]

48

**Table 3.** Water and sanitation in Yemen

| | 1990 | 2000 | 2012 |
|---|---|---|---|
| Population (x 1000) | 11,790 | 17,523 | 23,852 |
| Urban population (percentage) | 21 | 26 | 33 |
| **Use of sanitation facilities – urban (percentage of the population)** | | | |
| Improved | 70 | 82 | 93 |
| Unimproved – shared | 1 | 2 | 2 |
| Unimproved – other | 23 | 12 | 3 |
| Unimproved – open defecation | 6 | 4 | 2 |
| **Use of sanitation facilities – rural (percentage of the population)** | | | |
| Improved | 12 | 24 | 34 |
| Unimproved – shared | 1 | 2 | 3 |
| Unimproved – other | 33 | 32 | 32 |
| Unimproved – open defecation | 54 | 42 | 31 |
| **Use of sanitation facilities – total (percentage of the population)** | | | |
| Improved | 24 | 39 | 53 |
| Unimproved – shared | 1 | 2 | 3 |
| Unimproved – other | 31 | 27 | 22 |
| Unimproved – open defecation | 44 | 32 | 22 |
| **Use of drinking water sources –urban (percentage of the population)** | | | |
| Improved – total | 96 | 83 | 72 |
| Improved – piped on premises | 84 | 77 | 71 |
| Improved – other | 12 | 6 | 1 |
| Unimproved – other | 3 | 16 | 27 |
| Unimproved – surface water | 1 | 1 | 1 |
| **Use of drinking water sources – rural (percentage of the population)** | | | |
| Improved – total | 59 | 52 | 47 |
| Improved – piped on premises | 12 | 20 | 26 |
| Improved – other | 47 | 32 | 21 |
| Unimproved – other | 34 | 41 | 47 |
| Unimproved – surface water | 7 | 7 | 6 |
| **Use of drinking water sources – total (percentage of the population)** | | | |
| Improved – total | 66 | 60 | 55 |
| Improved – piped on premises | 27 | 35 | 40 |
| Improved – other | 39 | 25 | 15 |
| Unimproved – other | 28 | 35 | 41 |
| Unimproved – surface water | 6 | 5 | 4 |

**Source:** WHO/UNICEF Joint Monitoring Programme (JMP) for Water Supply and Sanitation, "Yemen: Estimates on the use of water sources and sanitation facilities". Available from www.wssinfo.org/documents/?tx_displaycontroller[type]=country_files (accessed 2 April 2015).

## Box 6. Water resource management policies and laws in Yemen

**1981**: The High Water Council was established in the former Yemen Arab Republic, and took responsibility for the country as a whole to reduce competition between three ministries, namely the Ministry of Agriculture and Water Resources (extraction for irrigation and dam construction), the Ministry of Oil and Mineral Resources (estimating water resources) and the Ministry of Electricity and Water (urban water). The Council remained ineffective due to its paralysis, distrust and competition between the three institutions.

**1995**: The National Water Resources Authority was established as the main government agency responsible for water policy, planning and development. It remained ineffective, with water being a low priority of the Government. The Authority and its branches, as technical specialist entities, were mandated to plan, monitor, regulate and manage the water resources in the local, basin and subsector levels, while the Ministry of Water and Environment served as the supreme supervisory entity in the sector at the national level and was in charge of strategic planning, institutional frameworks and policy development. It was supposed to regulate drilling of wells, monitor water quality, raise awareness about the water crisis, and resolve conflicts about water.

**2001**: The General Authority for Rural Electricity and Water Supply was rebranded into the General Authority for Rural Water Supply Projects, an autocratic institution that was meant to be later privatized, shifting power away from central Government.

**2002**: The Water Law was passed; however, by-laws were still not yet agreed upon by all parties.

**2003**: The Ministry of Water and Environment, which was established as a result of the implementation of the Water Law, was supposed to have full authority over water management. However, the new Ministry faced significant opposition by the Ministry of Agriculture and Irrigation and powerful landowners. Within a week of its establishment, its mandate was restricted to cover just drinking water, thereby rendering it comparatively ineffective.

**2011 (February)**: The Water Law executive by-law was issued nine years after the law itself was passed and just as the uprising in the country was beginning to derail the Government's legitimacy. The by-laws gave the National Water Resources Authority the power it currently has, including a final say in solving water issues when local authorities are unable to do so, and the power to issue permits for constructing and deepening wells. The by-laws of the Water Law also sanctioned government subsidies for drip irrigation for all crops, with the exception of qat.

**2005-2009 (updated in 2008 for 2009-2015)**: The National Water Sector Strategy and Investment Programme aimed at providing a strategy to manage the sector and promote investment from within. According to Lackner (2014), the Strategy was created among the profession elite based on misguided assumptions that disregard/misconstrue key social and political issues. During a review after three years of implementation, it appeared that the reforms worsened the situation for the poor by increasing poverty and making access to water more costly. Nevertheless, the strategy was updated in 2008 with no policy modifications.

**2011 (January)**: The Presidential National Conference on Management and Development of Water Resources in Yemen produced the Sana'a Declaration on the Yemeni Water Partnership. It sought to achieve safe and affordable access to water and sanitation services. Further development on this was brought to a halt as a result of the uprising.

**2011 (January)**: A ministerial decree was issued for the water basins and regions management organization.

Source: H. Lackner, "Water scarcity: Why doesn't it get the attention it deserves?", in *Why Yemen Matters: A Society in Transition*, H. Lackner, ed. (Saqi Books, 2014).

### 4. Sana'a: A microcosm of Yemen

Sana'a is the capital of Yemen and the largest city in the country. It is located inland, some 2,200 metres above sea level, and surrounded by mountains. The changing dynamics of the city have already had dramatic effects on available water resources. The Sana'a Basin is an intermountain basin situated in the western highlands of Yemen, where the capital is located. The population of Sana'a continues to grow, which translates into concomitantly rising water consumption rates at an annual average of 4.2 per cent.[24]

The Government's largely skewed focus on urban areas in terms of providing essential public services (health, education, roads, etc.) and limited rural economic development has encouraged Yemenis to migrate to those areas. As a result of this pattern of rural-urban migration, Sana'a and other major cities in the country have undergone rapid expansion, causing the urban population to rise from 22 per cent in 1990 to 33 per cent in 2014. Sana'a faces the brunt of these changes, with a population growing at a rate of 5 per cent annually.[25] In addition to its internal migrant population, Sana'a is also a destination for many refugees and asylum-seekers from the Horn of Africa. The challenges of addressing these demographic changes in Sana'a have been complicated by the social and political upheaval persisting since 2011.

The population growth of the past 10 years has added pressure to already strained conditions within the capital. In 2004, there were reportedly 1.7 million residents, compared to the current estimate of well over 2.5 million, thereby making Sana'a one of the fastest growing cities in the world.[26] The Municipality has inadequately planned for this rapid population growth and has failed to invest in the infrastructure needed to cope with it.

In Sana'a, which is the seat of government, education and business sectors, urban poverty is still widespread. In total, 26 per cent of heads of households have obtained higher education, while only 21 per cent have completed secondary school, 21 per cent have completed primary school, 18 per cent have no formal schooling but can read and write, and 13 per cent are unable to read and write. There is no recent data on poverty in Sana'a, but an indication can be gleaned from national averages, with 54 per cent of families living under the poverty line and an unemployment rate of 36 per cent. Data on household debt show that 68 per cent of households in Sana'a are in debt or have credit to repay, mostly for purchasing food and paying for health expenses. Data on food insecurity further illustrate this disadvantage: 20 per cent of the population reported regular food scarcity, while 8 per cent reported severe food scarcity. In parallel, 38 per cent of the population is reportedly chronically malnourished, 10 per cent of the population experiences acute malnourishment, 25 per cent are underweight, and 20 per cent of mothers are malnourished.[27]

The entire population of Sana'a is vulnerable to water scarcity. Water consumption in Sana'a increased from 4.5 billion cubic metres in 1990 to 13 billion cubic metres just 10 years later. Meanwhile, only 20 per cent of Yemen's groundwater is renewable and water levels are dropping by six metres a year in the Sana'a Basin, resulting in an annual deficit of 200 million cubic metres.[28] However, given the low socioeconomic status, some parts of the Governorate are more vulnerable owing to the high price matching and high demand for water in Sana'a. Those who are arguably the most vulnerable to water scarcity are residents of informal settlements in and around the city.

### 5. Informal settlements in and around Sana'a

New urban residents are typically forced to seek residence in informal areas or gatherings, to the extent that 67 per cent of Yemen's urban residents are living in informal settlements. These slums (and peri-urban informal settlements) are characterized by either old, deteriorated structures within the urban fabric, or newly constructed units that lack durability and are deprived of basic services.[29] The Municipality defines these informal settlements as "areas in which land is squatted on or subdivided without following an official subdivision plan and which are informally developed without adhering to any official planning and building regulations".[30]

In 2009, approximately 390,000, or about 20.5 per cent of the city's population, resided in informal settlements.[31] There are at least 35 informal settlements in Sana'a, with four communities close to the city centre and the rest scattered on the periphery. The Municipality has designated four types of informal settlements, namely slum pockets; informal areas within or near the core urban built-up area; informal areas on the far urban fringe (alongside or close to major roads or village extensions); and informal areas on land that was reserved for either the preservation of public goods or non-residential purposes.[32] Map 3 provides a satellite image of Sana'a, outlining the locations of these settlements in and around the city. Many of these communities are located on treacherous terrain, which constitutes an additional obstacle for city planners in terms of providing resources and infrastructure to these settlements. Table 4 highlights the types and features of informal settlements in Sana'a, and figure 10 shows population distribution by types of informal settlements.

**Map 3.** Locations of informal settlements within and around Sana'a City

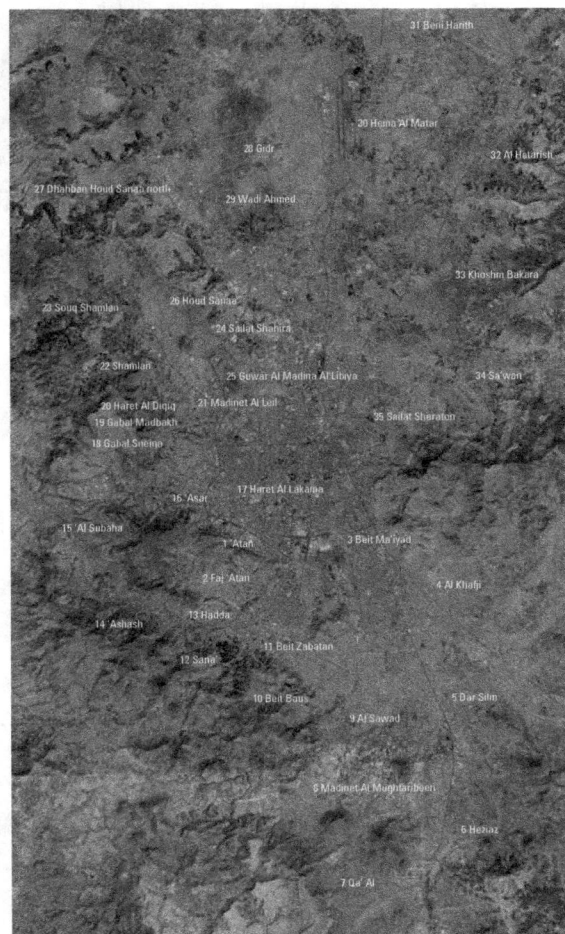

**Source:** El Shorbagi, Monica (2008). *Sana'a City Development Strategy – Urban Upgrading Study – Informal Residential Development and Informal Areas in Sana'a – Inventory, Typology, Dynamics, Strategy and Action Plan – Final Report*, (Municipality of Sana'a, 2008) p. 9. Available from www.citiesalliance.org/sites/citiesalliance.org/files/CAFiles/Projects/Final_Upgrading_Strategy_with_Exec_Sum.pdf.

**Table 4.** Types and key features of informal settlements in Sana'a

| No. | Type | Land tenure | Building stock | Density | Number and name of areas | Year of establishment | Post-planned | |
|---|---|---|---|---|---|---|---|---|
| | | | | | | | Yes | No |
| 1 | Slum pockets | Squatters on State land | Predominantly precarious structures | Dense | (17) Haret Al Lakama (qa'at al-mu'tamarat) | 1985 | ✓ | |
| | | | | | (23) Souq Shamlan | 2005 | | ✓ |

52

| No. | Description | Land | Building | Density | Area | Year | | |
|---|---|---|---|---|---|---|---|---|
| 2 | Informal areas within or close to the core urban built-up area | Mainly squatters on State land, some plots in some areas on private (ex-) agricultural land or on State land that was appropriated through unclear mechanisms and is meanwhile traded informally | Mostly low cost buildings on small plots, built mainly by owner-builders who construct and expand their house gradually

In some areas more larger multistorey buildings and/or villas (most notably area (25), many larger buildings also in areas (3) and (35) | Medium dense to dense, rapidly filling up | (3) Beit Ma'yad | 1985 | | ✓ |
| | | | | | (18) Gabal Sneina | 1995 | ✓ | |
| | | | | | (19) Gabal Madbakh | 1995 | ✓ | ☆ |
| | | | | | (20) Haret Al Diqiq | 1995 | ✓ | |
| | | | | | (21) Madinet Al Leil | 1990 | ✓ | |
| | | | | | (24) Sa'ilat Shahira | 1995 | ✓ | |
| | | | | | (25) around Al Madina Al Libiya | 1995 | | ✓ |
| | | | | | (35) Sa'ilat Sheraton | 1995 | ✓ | ✓ |
| 3a. | | | Areas (7), (22): Mostly very small, single family houses that are built incrementally with some medium-sized multistorey buildings in between | Low to medium density | (7) Qa' Al Qaidi | 1995 | ✓ | ☆ |
| | | | | | (5) Dar Silm | 1990 | ✓ | |
| | | | | | (8) Madinet al mughtaribeen | 1990 | ✓ | |
| | | | | | (15) Subaha | 1990 | | ✓ |
| | | | | | (22) Shamlan | 1990 | ✓ | ☆ |
| | | | | | (28) Mantiqet Gidr | 1995 | ☆ | ✓ |
| 3b. | Informal areas on the far urban fringe

(a) alongside or close to major roads

(b) village extensions | Mainly private (ex-) agricultural land with encroachment on State land on hills adjacent to agricultural land (mahariq) | Areas (5), (8), (9), (15), (16), (28), (34): Mixture of smaller, single-family houses and consolidated medium-sized multistorey buildings

Areas (10), (11), (12), (13, (14): Mainly medium-sized multistorey extended family houses mixed with larger, costly buildings and villas and small, single-family houses | | (6) around Heziaz village | 1995 | ✓ | |
| | | | | | (9) around Sawad village | 1995 | ✓ | |
| | | | | | (10) around Beit Baus village | 1990 | | ✓ |
| | | | | | (11) around Beit Zabatan village | 1995 | | ✓ |
| | | | | | (12) around Sana' village | 1995 | | ✓ |
| | | | | | (13) around Hadda village | 1990 | ☆ | ✓ |
| | | | | | (14) around 'Ashash village | 1990 | ✓ | ☆ |
| | | | | | (16) around 'Asar village | 1995 | ✓ | ☆ |
| | | | | | (34) Sa'wan village extension | 1995 | ✓ | ☆ |

| | | | | | | | | |
|---|---|---|---|---|---|---|---|---|
| **4a.** | Informal areas on land that was reserved for (a) the preservation of public goods (water resources and security of airport) (b) other non-residential purposes | Areas under (4a): Mainly squatters on State land with few plots on private land Areas under (4b): Informal construction on private (ex-) agricultural land on which construction is explicitly forbidden | Areas (4), (2), (26), (27), (29): mainly small, low-cost houses with some precarious structures and some medium-sized buildings in between Areas (1), (30), (31), (32), (33): Mixture of small, single-family and medium-size extended family houses with few larger, more costly buildings (particularly area (33)) | High density only area (4) Other areas low to medium density | (1) 'Atan | 1990 | ✓ | ☆ |
| | | | | | (2) Faj 'Atan | 1990 | ✓ | ☆ |
| | | | | | (4) Al Khafji | 1990 | ✓ | |
| **4b.** | | | | | (26) Sana'a water basin south | 1990 | | ✓ |
| | | | | | (27) Dhahban/ Sana'a water basin north | 1990 | | ✓ |
| | | | | | (29) Wadi Ahmed | 1995 | ✓ | ☆ |
| | | | | | (30) Hema Al Matar (east Salal Str.) | 1990 | | ✓ |
| | | | | | (31) Beni Al Harith | 1990 | ☆ | ✓ |
| | | | | | (32) Al Hatarish | 1985 | | ✓ |
| | | | | | (33) Khoshm Al Bakra (south Marib Rd.) | 1990 | | ✓ |

**Source:** Adapted from M. El-Shorbagi, *Sana'a City Development Strategy*.
**Notes:** "Post-planned" (last column) is defined as such in the source: "The main instrument of government response [to informal settlements] is an ex-post planning mechanism, i.e. the preparation and approval of detailed neighbourhood plans (mukhatatat wahdat algawar) that consist of the street layout and location of basic services such as a school, a mosque and a garden. These detailed plans are not embedded in any broader structural planning or strategic vision and are usually not enforced. In practice, most post-planned areas look virtually the same as unplanned areas and planners themselves use the term of "takhtit 'ashwa'i" (random planning) which reflects the fact that development in post-planned areas continues largely informally". (See M. El-Shorbagi, *Sana'a City Development Strategy*, p. 5.)
A tick (✓) denotes a majority; and a star (☆) denotes a minority.

Many of the urban poor in Sana'a are concentrated in these informal settlements that lack access to basic neighbourhood infrastructure and other life-enabling resources. According to El-Shorbagi, the main problems facing informal settlements are the lack of infrastructure and utilities, environmental problems and health hazards (for example, water pollution, pest infestations and exposed sewage), limited access to social services (for example, schools and health-care facilities), unsecured land rights, and dangers posed by difficult topography (for example, development in mountainous areas or along flood plains).[33] In terms of basic infrastructure and much like the rest of Sana'a, where connection to public water and sanitation is inconsistent, none of the informal settlements are connected to a public water source, and only 2 out of the total of 35 are connected to a public sewerage source.

**Figure 10.** Types of informal areas in Sana'a

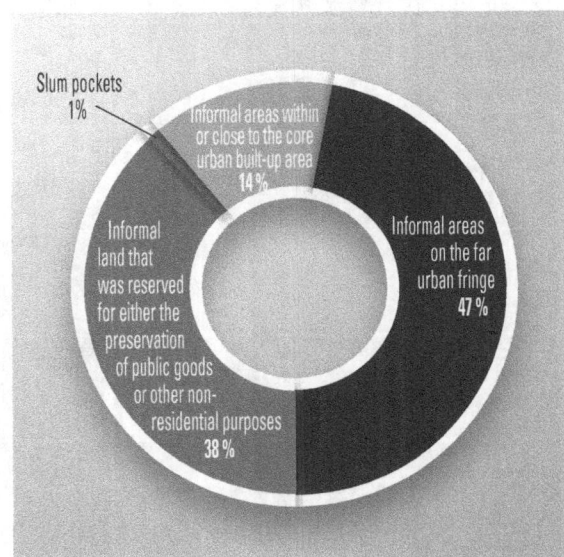

Slum pockets 1%
Informal areas within or close to the core urban built-up area 14%
Informal areas on the far urban fringe 47%
Informal land that was reserved for either the preservation of public goods or other non-residential purposes 38%

**Source:** M. El-Shorbagi, *Sana'a City Development Strategy*.

The majority of the informal settlements, however, are connected to a public network for electricity. Though, typically, the public system only partially covers these neighbourhoods, with many households extending electricity cables informally.[34] Many of these informal connections are hazardous, with poor quality cables hanging ubiquitously. Moreover, local energy distribution networks are overburdened and power outages are common (for a full description of the infrastructure of the informal areas, see table 5 below).

**Table 5.** Basic infrastructure in informal areas of Yemen

| Name of area | Source of water | | | Sewerage | | | Electricity | | | Street paving | |
|---|---|---|---|---|---|---|---|---|---|---|---|
| | Public network | Water tanker | Private well | Public network | Bayara (cesspit) | Open hole | Public network | Informal (rigged) | No access | Paved | Not paved |
| 'Atan | | ✓ | | | ✓ | | ✓ | ☆ | | ☆ | ✓ |
| Faj 'Atan | | ✓ | | | ✓ | | ✓ | ☆ | | ☆ | ✓ |
| Beit Maiyad | | ✓ | ☆ | ✓ | | | ✓ | | | ☆ | |
| Al Khafji | | ✓ | | | ✓ | | ✓ | | | | ✓ |
| Dar Slim | | ✓ | ☆ | | ✓ | | ✓ | | | ☆ | ✓ |
| Heziaz | | ✓ | | | ✓ | | ✓ | ☆ | | ☆ | ✓ |
| Qa' Al Qaidi | | ✓ | | | ✓ | | ✓ | | | | ✓ |
| Madinet al Mughtaribeen | | ✓ | | | ✓ | | ✓ | | | | ✓ |
| Sawad (village extension) | | ✓ | | | ✓ | | | ✓ | | | ✓ |
| Beit Baus (village extension) | | ✓ | | | ✓ | | ✓ | ☆ | | | ✓ |
| Zabatan (village extension) | | ✓ | ☆ | | ✓ | | ✓ | | | | ✓ |
| Sana' (village extension) | | ✓ | ☆ | | ✓ | | ✓ | ☆ | | | ✓ |
| Hadda (village extension) | | ✓ | ☆ | | ✓ | | ✓ | | | | ✓ |
| 'Al-Eshash (village extension) | | ✓ | | | ✓ | | ✓ | ☆ | | ☆ | ✓ |
| Al Subaha | | ✓ | ☆ | | ✓ | | ✓ | ☆ | | | ✓ |
| 'Asar (village extension) | | ✓ | ☆ | | ✓ | | ✓ | | | | ✓ |
| Haret Al Lakama | | ✓ | | | ✓ | | | ✓ | | | ✓ |

| | | | | | | | | | | | |
|---|---|---|---|---|---|---|---|---|---|---|---|
| **Gabal Sneina** | | ✓ | | | | ✓ | | ✓ | | | | ✓ |
| **Gabal Madhbah** | | ✓ | | | | ✓ | | | ✓ | | | ✓ |
| **Haret Al Diqiq** | | ✓ | | | | ✓ | | ✓ | ☆ | | | ✓ |
| **Madinet Al Leil** | | ✓ | | ✓ | | ✓ | | ✓ | | | ☆ | ✓ |
| **Shamlan** | | ✓ | ☆ | | | ✓ | | ✓ | ☆ | | | ✓ |
| **Souq Shamlan** | | ✓ | | | | | ✓ | | | ✓ | Tent – beside street |
| **Sailat Shahira** | | ✓ | | | | ✓ | | ✓ | ☆ | | | ✓ |
| **Next to Al Madina Al Libiya** | | ✓ | | | | ✓ | | ✓ | | | | ✓ |
| **Houd Sana'a south** | | ✓ | ☆ | | | ✓ | | ✓ | ☆ | | | ✓ |
| **Houd Sana'a north** | | ✓ | ☆ | | | ✓ | | ✓ | | | | ✓ |
| **Jadir area** | | ✓ | | | | ✓ | | ✓ | ☆ | | | ✓ |
| **Wadi Ahmed** | | ✓ | | | | ✓ | | ✓ | ☆ | | | ✓ |
| **Hema Al Matar** | | ✓ | | | | ✓ | | ✓ | ☆ | | | ✓ |
| **Beni Harith** | | ✓ | ☆ | | | ✓ | | ✓ | ☆ | | | ✓ |
| **Al Hatarish** | | ✓ | ☆ | | | ✓ | | ✓ | | | ✓ | * |
| **Khoshm Al Bakara** | | ✓ | ☆ | | | ✓ | | ✓ | ☆ | | | ✓ |
| **Mantiqet Sa'wan** | | ✓ | | | | ✓ | | | ✓ | | | ✓ |
| **Sailat Sheraton** | | ✓ | | ✓ | | | | ✓ | | | | ✓ |

**Source:** Adapted from El-Shorbagi, *Sana'a City Development Strategy*, p. 39.
**Note:** A tick (✓) denotes a majority and a star (☆) denotes a minority.

Informal settlements are usually developed on vacant, State-owned land, and housing is typically constructed with non- or semi-permanent materials.[35] Most informal settlement construction takes place without permits and accompanying infrastructure, thereby creating environmental conditions that are not conducive to the health and well-being of residents (box 7).[36] While a number of options have proved efficient in other countries, such as slum upgrading (including water supply and sanitation) or planning for future low-income settlements, the State has so far been unable to reign in rapid development in these areas, or to provide affordable housing to migrants and the urban poor. Meeting the development needs of these communities must go further than addressing the current settlements; they need to address longer-term development dynamics that

**Box 7.** Neighbourhood conditions in the informal settlement of Mahwa Aser in Sana'a

Residents of Mahwa Aser suffer from poor housing and an unhealthy living environment. They live in very small, one-floor dwellings with roofs of non-permanent materials. Some live in shacks made from plastic, metal sheets or cardboard. Only very narrow alleys exist between houses, which are not accessible by car. One part of Mahwa Aser has caught fire several times, which has prompted the State to relocate residents from that area for safety reasons. Inhabitants were safely relocated to Sawad Sa'awan resettlement project.

Mahwa Aser lacks sanitation - what is available is predominantly by pit latrine - and harbours dangerous diseases in the rainy seasons. The area also lacks clean water, which, when supplied, is made available for purchase by private vendors by tanker and container; electricity, which, when available, is usually rigged informally from nearby areas; paved streets and health and educational services.

**Source:** W.M.S. al-Daily, "An exploration of State and non-State actor engagement in informal settlement governance in the Mahwa Aser neighborhood and Sana'a City, Yemen", PhD dissertation, Virginia Polytechnic Institute and State University, 2013.

recognize the underlying factors that lead to the growth of these settlements.[37]

Recent internal migrants have reported that they have been driven to migrate for various reasons, including economic motivators (such as lack of employment, small size of land holdings, lack of access to water and reduction in agriculture production); societal and household pressure (such as disagreements between wives and mothers-in-law); lack of access to social services (quality education); and poor access to humanitarian organizations.[38] While many migrants arrive in Sana'a hoping to find work and a better life, they are instead met with unemployment or low-wage employment, which makes them reliant on humanitarian organizations for assistance.[39] Residents of low economic status in informal communities are also the most vulnerable to water scarcity, given that their neighbourhoods are often disconnected from public services and infrastructure.

The environmental and neighbourhood conditions described above are not conducive to the health and well-being of residents, many of whom are poor and/or recent migrants to the city and who, consequently,

are isolated and vulnerable to structural violence from indirect policy mechanisms that undermine the settlements (for example, withholding resources and services) to more direct forms of harassment and attack from the police or other agencies.[40]

Interviews with residents in Mahwa Aser have revealed that the Government refused to develop basic infrastructure in many parts of the settlement as a strategy to limit housing expansion and encourage resettlement elsewhere. Moreover, residents have received very little aid from the Government and NGOs, with local community leaders and governmental powerbrokers hoarding these resources as they were provided.[41]

These governmental forms of neglect and antagonism are related to the social marginalization of settlement residents, who are often members of lower caste groups and include refugees and asylum-seekers; *akhdam* (the *akhdam* are an ethnic minority in Yemen, considered of low social standing; the singular, *khadem*, means "servant" in Arabic); and other poor and marginalized groups. Residents of informal settlements have difficulty in claiming their rights and interests, as they cannot access patronage networks and lack mechanisms to express their voice. In order to address the needs of these communities, the Government needs to change its attitude towards residents from one of neglect and antagonism to one of support and inclusivity. However, changing these attitudes is particularly difficult given that they are entrenched in long-standing social practices and contemporary power dynamics that favour powerful local interests.[42]

## 6. The water crisis in Sana'a

The changing dynamics of the city have had dramatic effects on available water resources. Fears over water availability are particularly acute in Sana'a, where a rapidly expanding population coupled with rapidly declining water reserves result in a dire situation.[43] As

mentioned above, annual water consumption rates are growing at an average of 4.2 per cent, which results from population expansion as well as from illegal drilling, mainly water that is diverted for the production of qat and poor enforcement of conservation regulations. At this rate, groundwater wells serving Sana'a may dry by the next decade (map 5).[44]

In 2012, 71 per cent of the capital's residents reported access to improved water supplies, representing an increase from 41 per cent in 2007.[45] Residents of Sana'a receive their water from a variety of sources: 39 per cent receive their water from piped sources, 25 per cent from bottled water, and another 29 per cent from water tankers or other mobile merchants.[46] This diversity poses logistical challenges in terms of monitoring, regulation and

**Map 4.** Mean annual rainfall in millimetres across the Sana'a Basin

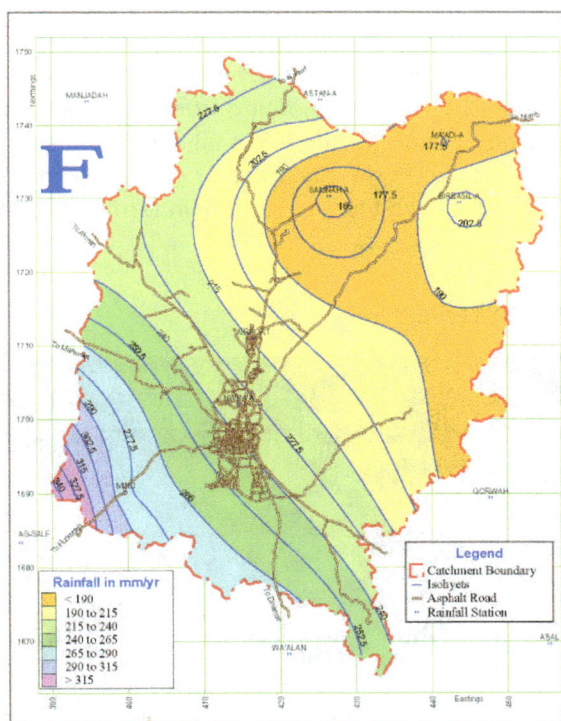

**Source:** Sana'a University Water and Environment Centre, *The Sana'a Basin Study, Volume 1, Main Report* (Sana'a, 2004). Available from http://www.yemenwater.org/?p=4803.

**Map 5.** Illustration of wells in the Sana'a Basin catchment area

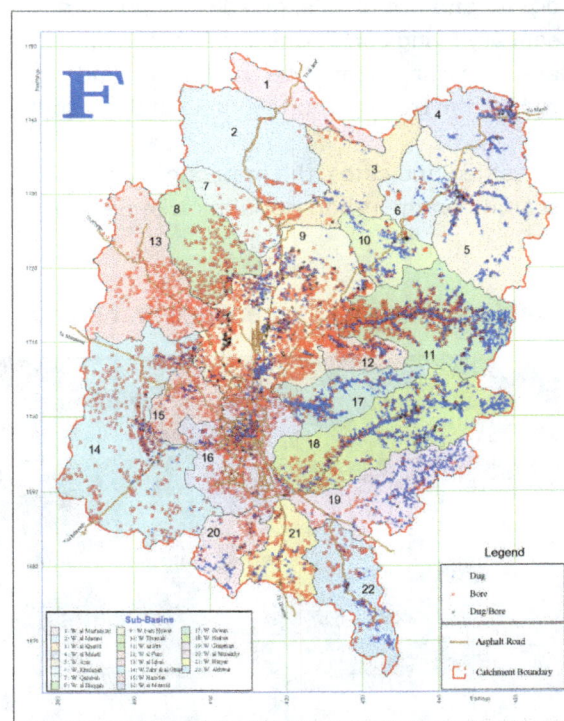

**Source:** Sana'a University Water and Environment Centre, *The Sana'a Basin Study.*

development. Improvements to the city's water supply must consider and support a diffuse set of service providers throughout the city and its outlying areas.

Declining water resources will impact the health of Sana'a residents. The lack of domestic supply leaves families, especially children, vulnerable to "life-threatening diseases, dangerously low water consumption levels and very poor sanitation standards and hygiene practices, in the home and at school".[47] It is estimated that 50 to 55 per cent of Sana'a is connected to public sewage, while the rest relies on individual solutions, which negatively affects the underground water reservoir.[48] The combination of dwindling domestic water resources with poor access to sanitation is a catalyst for enteric illnesses that drive malnourishment rates upwards. Undernourishment of children under 5 is closely associated to maternal malnutrition and low birth weight, which are strongly correlated to high rates of diarrhoea.[49] Improving access and use of safe, piped drinking water, sanitary living conditions and hygiene practices are necessary to improve child health and reduce the under-5 mortality rate of 6 per cent.[50]

As table 6 indicates, the impact of water scarcity on the urban population of Sana'a varies according to socioeconomic status and life circumstances. Sana'a, like many major cities, has significant wealth inequalities that ultimately dictate people's access to basic goods and services. Importantly, water scarcity affects sub-populations of the city differently, with the most vulnerable being refugees, asylum seekers, IDPs, migrants and, more broadly, poor residents in informal settlements. As groundwater resources run out, those in the informal settlements are most immediately affected. Small-scale farmers in the Sana'a Governorate are also vulnerable given that groundwater, which represents their main source of income, is depleting at a faster pace with each passing year, which forces communities to relocate. However, for the city as a whole, including informal settlements, it would be easy to secure the drinking water source by reallocating 5-10 per cent of the irrigation share in the basin to the domestic supply. Some physical investments and economic incentives are needed to apply this solution. Residents of informal settlements already face difficulties accessing potable water, with only 13 of the city's 35 informal neighbourhoods benefiting from direct access to water wells. Some informal communities are located in remote areas or on land with poor accessibility, particularly in terms of road

**Table 6.** Relationship between water and wealth in Yemen

| | Well off | Poor | Very poor |
|---|---|---|---|
| Water source for agriculture | Tube-well; spring; terraces; spate | Shared tube-well; spring; terraces; spate tail end; water purchase | No access |
| Use of diesel | Yes | Limited | No |
| Average per capita daily consumption | > 40 litres per day | 10-40 litres per day | Limited |
| Time spent fetching water | Nil | .. | Several hours each day, for women and girls |
| Cost of water per cubic metre (if purchased) | .. (operating cost of source) | Low for network supply; high for vendor supply | Very high, if purchased |

**Source:** Adapted from C. Ward and others, *Yemen's Water Sector Reform Program: A Poverty and Social Impact Analysis* (Republic of Yemen, GTZ and the World Bank, 2007).

**Box 8.** Vulnerability and local community response in Sana'a: the story of Omaimah, Amjad and Ossama

Securing water in Sana'a has become a daily struggle, particularly for the impoverished communities residing in the slums at the outskirts of the city. Omaimah is a mother of six children who describes the lack of reliable access to water as "living with our souls hanging between the earth and the heavens". While her family has been saving to buy a proper water tank as a strategic reserve, one that would allow them to buy water from water tanker trucks, every time they economize almost enough money, there is always an emergency which exhausts whatever savings they have.

Omaimah's and many families like hers are acutely aware of the water crisis in Yemen. This plight of the residents of Sana'a is becoming more noticeable, with an increasing number of families in need of water queuing for water longer than ever. Until they can afford it, they will have to continue relying on small water barrels, which the family has to send someone to fill on a regular basis. "We put empty containers on the wheelbarrow and someone has to go to the community tanker to queue and fill them up. Sometimes when no one is around to go we ask a neighbour to help out and we do the same. On occasion, my [12-year-old] son Amjad has to queue all day to fill up the containers, and many times he comes back empty-handed when the local tankers are empty".

One time, Amjad was beaten for filling up containers from a mosque as he was accused of stealing water from there. When the situation is absolutely dire, Omaimah now resorts to sending her younger children with small containers because she believes they will be less likely to get hit.

Osama is a young person who has decided to take action in response to this plight. He and a number of youth volunteers have engaged in efforts to raise resources, procure water in water tankers and deliver them to vulnerable communities, including to Omaimah's family. Osama considers the work to be a "lifeline for many people, a great responsibility and a lot of pressure for the small group of volunteers. If we get busy or delayed in delivering water, we feel like we have let people down and so we do our best".

Osama says it would be unimaginable what would happen to such vulnerable families if he and people like him had not stepped up to help, he is happy to report that he has not ran short of funding and many such groups are emerging to help the most vulnerable, even during the current times of crisis.

**Source:** Personal communication with Osama Abdullah, volunteer for Yemeni Youth for Humanitarian Relief, 4 June 2015.

infrastructure and for providing passage for water tankers. As a result, residents pay higher prices or must collect water on foot.[51]

The poor regulation of groundwater has resulted in the over-abstraction and intensive depletion of the basin aquifers and, moreover, has led to deteriorating water quality and a rise in the cost of finding clean water for household consumption.[52] Additionally, residents of Sana'a use groundwater sources that are polluted by nitrates from the sewage plant,

cesspits and agriculture. These conditions disproportionately affect the poor, and particularly residents in informal settlements, who have less access to community infrastructure and resources.[53]

In fact, there are large gaps between the rich and poor in accessing improved water sources. Specifically, only 2 per cent of people in the poorest households have improved access, compared to 77 per cent of those living in the richest households.[54] Moreover, the time spent collecting water by poor households without water on premises averages 76.6 minutes. In general, adult females collect water when the source of drinking water is not on the premises (68.2 per cent). Adult men collect water in only 11.4 per cent of cases; and children under the age of 15 collect water in 15.9 per cent of cases, with the task being completed by girls about 60 per cent of the time.[55] Such poor access to water has detrimental consequences for children: an estimated 50 per cent of deaths of children under the age of 5 can be attributed to diarrhoea. Furthermore, women and girls spend large parts of each day fetching water, which impacts their ability to participate in education and labour markets.[56]

## 7. Recommendations for overcoming vulnerability to water scarcity in Sana'a

Both international development agencies and local authorities are struggling to address the water scarcity situation in Sana'a. Many of the local realities are obstacles to change: Yemen's poverty, frail governmental institutions and oligarchic political economy defined by self-interest and patronage all contribute to the failure of national policies.[57] Moreover, conflicting local interest groups and an ongoing civil war that further exacerbates local conflicts are an impediment to sustainable development. Yemen's decision-making apparatus is heavily influenced from outside the traditional State apparatus, with substantial political sway in the hands of powerful farming sheikhs.[58] State institutions, such as the Ministry of Water and Environment and the National Water Resources Authority, are relatively young and have been unable to exert influence to reform the management of water supply. Improvements should be made, particularly given the dwindling supply of groundwater and the dire projections that the city will run out of water in the coming years.[59]

The city's basic infrastructure and public sector capacity is already overstretched, and the current turmoil threatens to prolong instability and inefficiencies of governmental institutions. Yemen is a poor country, and political instability discourages local and foreign investment in long-term development. The people who suffer most from turmoil are the country's rural and urban poor, whose living conditions are exacerbated by conflict. Discussions on sustainable development may seem academic and far-fetched against the backdrop of ongoing armed conflict and tensions across the country. However, once the political situation in Sana'a and the rest of the country stabilizes, there will be a need to consider the following recommendations:

(a) **Respecting the local context:** Addressing water management needs in Sana'a requires context-specific and culturally sensitive policies. There have been numerous attempts by foreign development agencies to initiate "fix-it" projects that have either had a marginal impact or have been totally unsuccessful. For example, in 2003, the World Bank developed the Sana'a Basin Water Management Project aiming at countering water scarcity in the city area. In evaluating its project, the World Bank attributed water scarcity in the basin to expanded irrigation needs for cash crops.[60] However, the report did not contextualize the expansion of irrigation as a by-product of international development policies that promote cash-crop industries and that are environmentally unsustainable. Instead, the report attributed the project's limited sustainable impact to a lack of buy-in from government officials. That case is emblematic of the limitations of international development approaches in addressing water scarcity in Yemen.

(b) **Making more water available for urban centres:** A sustainable development approach to addressing water scarcity needs to tackle the root causes of precarious environmental and living conditions, or else it will fail to alleviate the population's vulnerability to water scarcity.

This approach should seek ways to improve State governance capacities and contribute to internal stability. It must anticipate and address rural-to-urban migration either by strengthening resource development in rural areas or by dedicating more resources to planned urban development. While development policy has been promoting the allocation of water resources to agriculture, the surge in migration to urban centres paired with declining water resources requires earmarking more water for domestic consumption.[61]

**(c) Redefining the role of the public sector:** Currently, the Government plays a limited role in terms of addressing water scarcity issues and providing water management systems. The role of the public sector should be redefined to develop an enabling framework that encompasses a number of responsibilities, including the responsibility to expand existing examples of effective programmes and projects; to systematically engage stakeholders in the community management of groundwater resources; and to regulate quality, pricing and planning of land use. The Government should organize support for community-based water governance processes. Ultimately, it should be the Government's responsibility to integrate public assistance programmes with community efforts.[62]

**(d) Empowering local people:** There are two divergent approaches to development in the literature. The first, both conventional and unproven, is characterized by empowering government agencies, encouraging technological innovation and building greater consensus on the need for policy change. This approach has been characterizing the status quo for decades, and there is little evidence of success to support its continuation. Since the Yemeni uprisings of 2011, it has been increasingly untenable. The second approach emphasizes the need for water

policies to rely on local people and on their knowledge, resourcefulness and self-interest to spearhead change. Indeed, local people affected by water scarcity – in this particular case, urban slum dwellers – must be at the heart of all development programmes and initiatives aimed at addressing water scarcity.

Rather than positing the Government as the focal point of water management, the emphasis should be on bolstering local actors.[63] Accordingly, international development agencies should consider prioritizing local solutions while developing partnerships whereby the local population plays a leading role. International development agencies should also concentrate their efforts on building consensus among financial stakeholders to follow the same basic rules, regulations and incentive system. Their planning should take place at the basin-level along with the local-district level governance structures. Moreover, the rural poor in agriculture need to be prioritized in order to advocate a "more income per drop" framework that benefits the most vulnerable.[64]

**(e) Involving residents in decision-making processes:** Policymakers should be challenged to consider how political processes exclude and further marginalize the most disadvantaged communities, and how implementation strategies might disproportionately benefit specific interest groups. In Sana'a, the most disadvantaged residents of the informal settlements are most affected by water scarcity and its consequences. Yet, most policies and programmes appear to benefit primarily other, less disadvantaged communities in the city. Specifically, the Government has adopted an antagonistic attitude towards these settlements, viewing them as an obstacle to planned development. Interestingly, many of the reports on informal settlements barely mention the residents themselves, as though they are invisible or irrelevant to the policymaking process.[65] This invisibility should change. Moreover, residents should be involved in planning that incorporates economic and social development with infrastructural development in a constructive manner.[66]

## B. Landless and small farmers of the Jordan Valley and refugees and their host community in Mafraq, Jordan

### 1. Population indicators

For centuries, population settlements in Jordan have been concentrated in the rain-fed highlands and in the fertile Jordan Valley, leaving much of the arid regions sparsely populated. In the past 50 years, communities spread considerably in the Jordan Valley with the arrival of Palestinian refugees and improved irrigation techniques. Natural population growth, migration, improved irrigation techniques and road networks led to the settling of communities in areas where average annual rainfall is below 250 mm, as well as towards the east, with the proliferation of well drilling, in the areas of Mafraq and Azraq.

Despite its agricultural origins, Jordan's population is now mainly urban, with half the national population concentrated within the Amman-Ruseifa-Zarqa conurbation (map 6). The northern governorates, with less desert areas, have densities of over 300 inhabitants per km², while Kerak and Tafila have suffered from population migrations towards the capital and have respective population densities of 68 and 39 inhabitants per km².[67] Jordan's population became significantly urbanized during the 1960s, reaching a rate of urbanization of over 80 per cent by 2011. The two main reasons were rural depopulation and the arrival of waves of Palestinian refugees and displaced persons who mostly settled in the larger towns of Amman, Zarqa, Irbid and Ruseifa, where camps

**Map 6.** Population density in Jordan, 2008

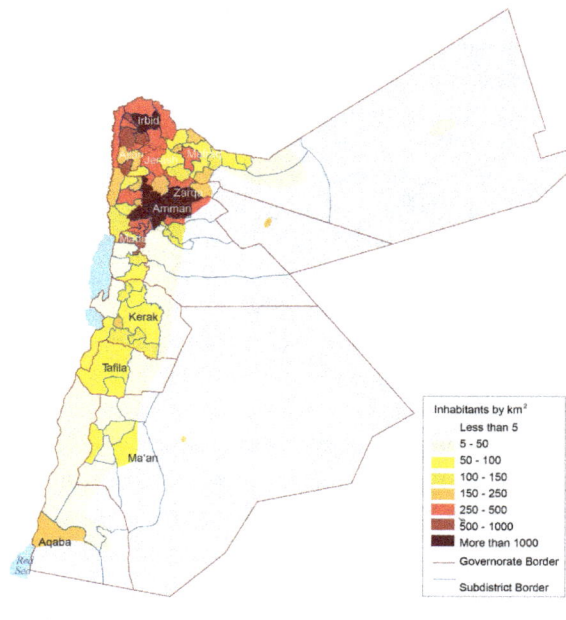

Source: M. Ababsa, "Changes in the regional distribution of the population", in *Atlas of Jordan* (Beirut: Presses de UIFPO, Institut français du Proche – Orient, 2013). Available from http://books.openedition.org/ifpo/5021?lang=en.

and services had been set up by the United Nations Relief and Works Agency for Palestine Refugees in the Near East (UNRWA). Migration movements from, to and through Jordan have continually played a key role in shaping its demographic situation as well as the economic and political structure. In both 1948 and 1967, Jordan received a great influx of Palestinian refugees. In 1991 and 2003, during the two Gulf wars, Jordan received about a million returnees from Kuwait and refugees from Iraq, respectively. Most recently, between 2011 and 2015, the crisis in the Syrian Arab Republic has resulted in approximately 1.1 million refugees, including some 600,000 registered with the Office of the United Nations High Commissioner for Refugees (UNHCR).

The population of Jordan is estimated to have reached 6.3 million in 2012[68] and is expected to double within the next 30 years, with 78 per cent being under the age of 30.[69] An unprecedented number of women are of reproductive age and fertility rates remain high, at 3.5 children per woman. Such rapid population growth is further exacerbating water scarcity in Jordan.

Approximately 37 per cent of Jordan's main surface water sources emerge from shared transboundary rivers: the Jordan and Yarmouk Rivers.[70] Jordan's shares of water allocations are governed by agreements with Israel and the Syrian Arab Republic, leaving Jordan uniquely vulnerable to interruptions to transboundary flows. The Zarqa River is largely polluted by industrial and municipal waste. Jordan also depends heavily on 12 renewable groundwater aquifers, representing 54 per cent of water supply, which are at critical stages of exploitation.[71] Groundwater abstraction takes place at more than twice the recharge rate,[72] and licensed and unlicensed wells contribute to overexploitation. For example, in the Azraq Basin, groundwater wells, of which an estimated 76 per cent are illegal, extract water at a rate of 247 per cent of sustainable yield.[73] The quantity of national water supply is about 900 million cubic metres per annum, while the quantity of water demand is about 1,200 million cubic metres across all sectors.[74] Water shortage in Jordan has long been identified as a critical constraint to its future development and the single most significant challenge to the next generation.[75]

Water in Jordan is closely tied to food, energy and urban development. Yet, the combined current economic and demographic pressures are leading to a crisis unlike any in the past. The declining water supply in the country owes to a great extent to the absence of a clear and efficient regulatory system for water, the subsidization of water that allows for inefficient water use, overexploitation of aquifers leading to increased salinity and dropping water tables. If supply remains constant, per capita domestic consumption is projected to fall to 90 cubic metres per year by 2025, putting Jordan in the category of absolute water shortage that could negatively impact the well-being of the population, endangering public health and constraining economic growth.[76]

Jordan faces the critical challenge of securing water to provide for its rapidly expanding population and to meet its growth aspirations. Jordan's water resources dilemma is two-fold: unregulated activities of a burgeoning population result in increasing water pollution; and increasing demands and competition over finite water supplies. On the one hand, the desire for food security and maintenance of livelihoods for rural populations has enabled an allocation of highly subsidized water to the agricultural sector, with 66 per cent of available water targeting low-value uses in agriculture, which contributes to only 3 per cent to GDP.[77] On the other hand, demand for domestic use for burgeoning urban populations and industrial uses, which generate higher returns on water use, has resulted in increased pressure for reallocation of scarce water resources.

Within that context, certain segments of the population face heightened vulnerability to water scarcity. This section focuses on impoverished refugee and host communities in urban Mafraq, and on landless and small farmers of the Jordan Valley. The two case studies were selected to showcase the competing needs of the rural/agricultural sector and its vulnerable populations of small holding and landless farmers; and the urban populations, particularly in economically disadvantaged and migration-stressed Mafraq. Owing to the sudden influx of refugees in the Governorate of Mafraq, approximately 60.5 per cent of the population is now Syrian, and the population of the city of Mafraq has increased by 128 per cent.[78] Water stress and risk levels of this already impoverished and vulnerable population have increased dramatically as a result of the loss of livelihoods and the increased costs of what were once affordable municipal water and sanitation services.[79]

Similarly, the rural population in the Jordan Valley faces increasing vulnerability to water

**Figure 11.** Poverty in Jordan

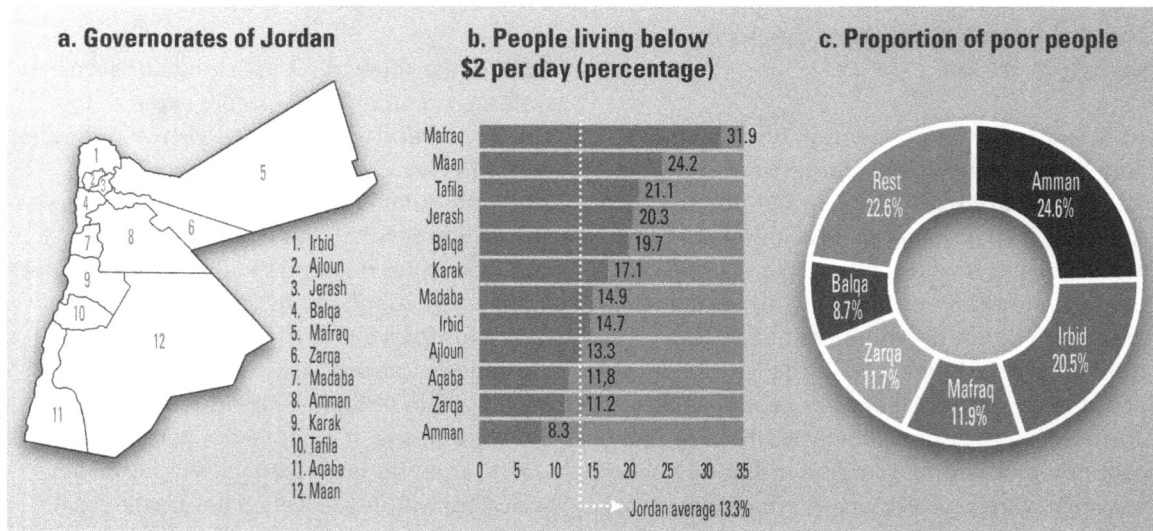

| a. Governorates of Jordan | b. People living below $2 per day (percentage) | c. Proportion of poor people |

Source: Jordan, Department of Statistics.

scarcity owing to a high concentration of agriculture, dependence on low-priced water as the primary input of production, and increasing water scarcity from both overextraction and increased pressure on finite water resources in other sectors and urban areas. This case study on Jordan takes a closer look at the impact of water scarcity on the Governorate of Mafraq, where the sudden influx of Syrian refugees has increased the income vulnerability of all inhabitants – Jordanian and Syrian – to water scarcity, as well as the small and landless farmers in the Jordan Valley, which constitutes the foundation for Jordan's food security and employment of a significant portion of the country's agricultural labour. Both populations represent the most underprivileged and vulnerable urban and rural groups, respectively, who are facing acute water stress, threatened livelihoods and changes in standards of living.

## 2. Availability and governance of water resources in Jordan

(a) Availability of water resources

Unconventional water production plays a large role in preserving groundwater, enabling Jordan to use brackish water after desalination. While desalination is now a necessity rather than an option, desalinated water contributes to a small albeit growing share of Jordan's water supply, and is expected to grow as a result of industrialization, accelerated urbanization, population growth and depletion of conventional water resources. Jordan is also increasingly using more treated municipal wastewater to meet escalating demand, especially in agriculture. Much of Amman's treated wastewater effluent is discharged in the Zarqa River and is impounded by the King Talal Dam, where it is blended with fresh floodwater and subsequently released for irrigation use in the Jordan Valley.[80] Treated wastewater is estimated at 121 million cubic metres a year and rising.[81] Wastewater treatment and reuse is shaped by water scarcity, financial capacity and the importance of the agricultural sector. In Jordan, treated wastewater combined with freshwater irrigate food crops on some 10,600 hectares, thereby providing some 20 per cent of the country's irrigation water.[82] Additionally, rainwater is harvested for irrigation and water supply, especially in the northern areas of Jordan which receive greater precipitation. Water harvesting techniques offer a necessary, low-tech solution to promoting water-use efficiency while minimizing environmental degradation. Increasingly, it is supported as a community-based initiative that can supplement water resources on small farms and households.

## (b) Water use

Water in Jordan is used mainly by agriculture, municipal/domestic uses and industry. Domestic water demand accounts for 33 per cent of total demand, while agriculture and industry account for 60 per cent and 7 per cent, respectively.[83] Key political, environmental and social drivers of water policy are determined by agricultural policy, energy use, desire for food security and self-sufficiency, land use policy, and pressures of rural-urban migration with its associated changes in demography and land use. Increasing competing pressures for water from agriculture and industry, in addition to mounting domestic demand stemming from population growth, are driving the Government to invest heavily in securing new water resources, pursue demand management initiatives, improve water governance and efficiencies, and increase agricultural reliance on treated wastewater.

There is a need to cap irrigation demand in order to satisfy municipal, industrial and tourism water demands.[84] Within the agricultural sector, most irrigation occurs in two distinct areas: the Jordan Rift Valley and the uplands.[85] Despite the scarcity of water, high water-consuming crops, such as tomatoes and bananas, are still being grown in Jordan. Moreover, water losses (non-revenue water) are at an alarming 46.8 per cent.[86] This amounts to some 76 billion litres per year, which could meet the needs of 2.6 million people.[87] Mafraq has the most inefficient system, with losses around 78 per cent,[88] resulting from a lack of law enforcement, very low penalties for the use of illegal water, an absence of individual

responsibility or awareness for water wastage among citizens, low maintenance of the pipes, and poor quality of pipe repair materials.[89]

Using groundwater resources beyond their natural replenishment rate has resulted in the rapid depletion of aquifer reserves, and salinization and deterioration in water quality. In the Amman-Azraq basin in Jordan, excessive abstraction has increased groundwater salinity from less than 400 milligrams per litre (mg/L) in 1994 to 1,800 mg/L in 2004 as a result of encroaching saltwater.[90] Overpumping groundwater also depletes national assets. While economic activities based on extracted water boost GDP in the short term, groundwater overexploitation, especially mining fossil water resources, erodes a country's natural capital and threatens irrigated areas in the long term. The value of national wealth consumed by overexploiting groundwater is estimated at as much as 2 per cent of GDP in Jordan.[91] These practices have triggered a chain of adverse impacts, such as an increase of water and soil salinity, decrease of the land productivity and depopulation of some areas.[92]

## (c) Access to water

In Jordan, 93.1 per cent of the population is connected to municipal water systems (water subscribers), of which 97.6 per cent are receiving their water once weekly; only 2.4 per cent of water subscribers receive their water on a daily basis. Wastewater subscribers represent only 78.7 per cent of total subscribers; and treated wastewater volume reached 134.5 million cubic metres in 2012, which was entirely used by agriculture.[93] A high rate of natural population growth combined with massive influxes of refugees have critically transformed the population water imbalance. A key reaction to abrupt increases in population has been overextraction of water from groundwater aquifers. It is estimated that 9 out of 12 ground water aquifers are overexploited.[94] The annual freshwater withdrawals exceeded 138 per cent of internal resources in 2011, and water tables are dropping by an average of 1 to 2 metres per year.[95] Jordan now draws heavily on non-renewable fossil aquifers (such as Disi Aquifer, which is shared between Jordan and Saudi Arabia) to offset the negative water balance. While a comparatively large share of the population has access to improved drinking water, access is not always reliable, especially in low-income areas. Water shortages are a major problem in such key cities as Amman and, increasingly, in northern cities of Jordan where water supply has been unable to keep up with population growth stemming from the sudden influxes of refugees.[96]

## (d) Water pricing and spending

Costs per delivered cubic metre of water in Jordan must take into account extraction, desalination, water treatment and energy costs associated with pumping water.[97] The energy costs associated with water extraction and conveyance are high, consuming 14 per cent of electricity produced in Jordan.[98] The energy costs of pumping water from groundwater aquifers for agricultural purposes represent 10 per cent of agricultural inputs.[99] Water pumped from Disi bears an estimated cost of 0.82 Jordanian dinars (JD) per cubic metre (approximately $1.16). The massive influx of Syrian refugees has put strong upward pressure on Jordan's energy bill. In fact, Jordan's energy consumption for the water sector was JD 53 million in 2010, rising to JD 62 million in 2011 and reaching JD 109 million by 2013 (approximately $74.7 million, $87.4 million and $153.7 million, respectively).[100] This translates into an annual increase of 17 per cent to 37 per cent. Desalination is estimated to cost JD 2 ($2.82) per cubic metre.

Despite these high costs, Government subsidies, representing 5 per cent of the national budget in 2010,[101] mean that water tariffs in Jordan are below their economic price, with the ratio to total cost coverage at

56 per cent in 2013.[102] As noted above, 1 cubic metre of water costs approximately $2.82, which incorporates extraction, treatment/disinfection, operation and maintenance. However, as a result of the heavily subsidized water tariff, customers pay on average less than $0.71 per cubic metre.[103] Even though the majority of the water is consumed by agriculture, farmers in the Jordan Valley pay only 10 per cent of total cost whereas households pay 50 per cent, thereby contributing to government deficits.[104] The full cost is only paid in the tourism sector.[105] The Water Authority of Jordan (WAJ) has operated under annual deficits of more than $50 million from 1990, which has reduced the Authority's net worth from $177 million in 1990 to zero by 1995. The Authority's inability to generate sufficient surplus to finance its investment programme has resulted in large debt obligations.[106] Moreover, the availability of inexpensive, heavily subsidized water provides little incentive for conservation, moving the argument towards more realistic and equitable pricing.

## (e) Water governance

While economic pricing may be the most effective method of ensuring conservation, a major governance issue is how to provide the public with adequate, inexpensive water. Balancing multiple water uses amid water scarcity and competing interests can generate social and economic problems. Since agriculture produces only a small share of GDP, its abandonment in favour of more productive sectors, such as heavy industry and tourism, could leave rural inhabitants impoverished and without livelihoods. This in turn could stimulate migration to the cities, thereby increasing socioeconomic pressure on overpopulated and poor urban areas that are inadequately served in terms of water.

Jordan has vital national and human security interests in finding a path to water sustainability, and has introduced water reforms over more than two decades. The water sector is highly centralized in the country, where the Government plays a dominant role. The Water Authority, which was created in 1983, holds overall responsibility for national drinking water supply and sanitation, while the Jordan Valley Authority, established in 1977, holds overall responsibility for irrigation management; and the Ministry of Water and Irrigation (MWI), founded in 1988, has overall responsibility for integrated water resource management and intersectoral coordination. There are often overlapping mandates between these three institutions, resulting sometimes in a lack of cohesiveness in water management.

Efforts to improve water governance include the development of a national water strategy (Water for Life 2008-2022) that incorporates many elements of integrated water resource management. Jordan has also taken steps to reform its legal system to formulate water quality management policies, specify required legal procedures and better define responsibilities in institutional frameworks. Legislatively, water laws have been implemented to support institutional reforms, such as Law 30/2001 to clarify the roles and responsibilities of the Jordan Valley Authority, Law 54/2002 on public health, Law 85/2002 to regulate groundwater usage, and Law 12/2003 on environmental protection.[107] However, the legal framework does not fully support the implementation of national water strategies.[108]

While efforts by reformists have produced a decline in agriculture's share of renewable water use to 66 per cent and have increased wastewater use, these efforts have not achieved the improvements required to protect aquifers and their water quality, or narrow worsening deficits.[109] Recognizing the extreme population vulnerability to water scarcity, Jordan's water strategy for 2009-2022 aims to invest JD 5.86 billion (approximately $8.26 billion) over 15 years, corresponding to more than 160 per cent of Jordan's GDP.[110]

A significant portion of that is to access unconventional and new sources of water, such as Disi and Red-Dead projects.

## 3. Jordan Valley

The Jordan Valley, which is also called the Jordan Rift Valley, stretches from the eastern side of the Jordan River Basin in the north to the Dead Sea. The Jordan Valley and Southern Ghor are among the most important agricultural areas thanks to a permanent source of water from the Yarmouk River and side dams for the former, and from surface water for the latter. Owing to its position below sea level and a microclimate with high temperatures, these two are the most important vegetable-producing areas in winter. Cultivable lands in Ghor total approximately 34,000 hectares, with the majority of holdings between 3 and 4 hectares.[111] The Valley produces about 40 per cent of total national agricultural production and 70 per cent of total national agricultural gross revenue.[112] However, the contribution of agriculture to national GDP has declined in relative terms from 20 per cent in 1974 to less than 2.9 per cent in 2011.[113] In the past two decades, industrial and other sectors have expanded and the contribution from agriculture as a percentage of GDP has decreased from 8.1 per cent in 1990, to 3.5 per cent in 1998, reaching 2.9 per cent of GDP in 2011. Despite the low contribution of agriculture to GDP, both rain-fed and irrigated agriculture remain vital socioeconomic activities in Jordan, especially the Jordan Valley. Employment in the agricultural sector is 5.5 per cent of the active labour force;[114] and nationally, that sector employs around half a million people and generates 14.5 per cent of total exports.[115]

Agricultural production in the Jordan Valley depends largely on irrigation. As a result of extensive infrastructural works, a comprehensive irrigation network was built centred on the King Abdullah Canal and a number of dams to feed it. The irrigated areas

68

are located in the Jordan Valley (some 33,000 hectares), and in the Plateau (some 44,100 hectares). Catchment areas for groundwater recharge are characterized by frequent water shortage and, as a result, abstraction rates are higher than recharge rates, which in turn increases the salinity of groundwater. The average decline of groundwater level was greatest in the Jordan Side Valleys basin, with a drop of 1.9 metres per year. Thus, the forecast average groundwater-level decline in this basin is about 38 meters by 2030.[116]

A high proportion of water used in agriculture produces low or no financial crop value. Returns on water investments in such crops as maize, barley, wheat and olives produce modest or even negative financial returns for farmers and their communities.[117] Much of agriculture production goes towards water-intensive crops, including tomatoes, bananas, wheat, and barley. Tomatoes, which are the most commonly grown vegetable in the Jordan Valley, require significantly more water than such crops as potatoes, squash, cauliflower, aubergine and watermelon, highlighting opportunities for water conservation through crop replacements. Tomatoes are currently subsidized for export to the Gulf region.[118]

(a) Demographic and socioeconomic characteristics of the local population

Farming in the Jordan Valley supports a significant number of communities, and the poor and lower classes are the first to feel the impact of water shortages and poor water quality. Some 350,000 people are the main beneficiaries of irrigated agriculture, and women form an important component of the agricultural labour force. Small-scale farmers are usually engaged in renting or sharecropping, often indebted to middlemen who market their products. The landless usually depend on wage labour and informal employment in rural areas as sharecroppers. In total, 50 per cent of casual labourers in Jordan are women.

Typically, households in the Valley tend to be large (6.6 persons per household), including small children and elderly parents, and often unemployed adults. According to a study conducted in 2012, an estimated 10 per cent of farmers in the Jordan Valley were illiterate;[119] and only 37.3 per cent of the population had obtained the high school diploma (tawjihi) in 2011, according to the Department of Statistics. The poverty rate in the Jordan Valley was 32.2 per cent in 2010 (figure 11), and unemployment stood at 14.2 per cent, which is higher than the national average of 12.9 per cent.[120] More than 70,000 people live in poverty in the Jordan Valley (representing 10 per cent of the poor at the national level), of which about 22,100 people are beneficiaries of the National Aid Fund. Incomes are very low, with many families lacking resources to pay for schooling or health care. According to the Department of Statistics, only 56 per cent of the population living in the Jordan Valley has health insurance.[121]

(b) Agricultural institutional framework

Land reform measures enacted in the Jordan Valley in the early 1960s redistributed land into farm units that could be efficiently irrigated by the new canal, and allowed more people to own and operate farms. State policy aimed at imposing an upper ceiling on holdings in order to narrow inequalities in land ownership.[122] In practice, the redistribution programme reduced the average land holding from 43 dunams to 21.3 dunams in the project area, while only 3.5 per cent of the owned farms were larger than 150 dunams after redistribution. At that time, more than 60 per cent of the farmers owned less than one unit (30 dunams) after redistribution. Moreover farmers were not allowed to sell their land directly to others, with only the Jordan Valley Authority serving as recognized buyer. However, 40 years of implementation of the land reform programme have resulted in high levels of fragmentation, caused by a successive subdivision of land due to inheritance, among other factors.[123]

By 2003, the Government adopted a new land reform programme that permitted beneficiaries to sell or buy other holdings without referring to the Jordan Valley Authority. By 2007, according to the agricultural census, 41.6 per cent of total crop surface in Jordan represented small holdings under 10 dunams and was owned by 95.3 per cent of farmers, while large properties over 100 dunams represented 26 per cent of the agricultural area and were owned by 0.4 per cent of farmers, mostly served by foreign labour. In 2010, the migrant labour force was an estimated 298,000 workers, of which 28.7 per cent (some 85,623 people) were engaged in the agricultural sector.[124] Jordan's rural communities lack both economic and water security, and these trends have motivated many to accept State buy-outs and to consider changes to other livelihoods. Moreover, as a result of land fragmentation and urban encroachment in agricultural areas, field and mainly grain/cereal crops have become less profitable and their management (for example, tillage operations) have become more difficult with shrinking farm sizes.[125]

The Jordan Valley Authority is responsible for the supply of bulk water needed for the irrigation of different crops. Water is a primary commodity that directly impacts the competitiveness and food security of small farmers. In the Jordan Valley, where agriculture depends on irrigation, farmers buy water at an average tariff of JD 0.012 ($0.17) per cubic metre, which is cheaper than the average paid by private farmers in the highlands. However, farmers pumping from private wells pay nothing for the first 150,000 cubic metres and then JD 0.005 ($0.007) per cubic metre between 150,000 and 200,000 cubic metre, and JD 0.060 ($0.085) per cubic metre thereafter. This pricing policy benefits large farmers as well as small farmers. Governments have been reluctant to press for demand management in the past because this would have involved confronting politically influential landowners.[126]

The availability of subsidized water resources to the agricultural sector is threatened by the need to allocate water to other, more productive sectors of the economy. In recent years, water consumption in agriculture has declined, especially in the Jordan Valley, owing to many factors, including the loss of irrigated farm area with persistent drought, economic competition in the agricultural sector from neighbouring countries and sectors, increased regulation of wells and implementation of new water saving technologies.[127] Increasing water scarcity in the Jordan Valley threatens to impact the livelihoods of the most vulnerable agriculture workers, namely the landless and small farming rural populations.

(c) Impact of water scarcity on the population in the Jordan Valley

Increasingly, the need to prioritize the municipal sector has resulted in channelling available surface water from the Jordan Valley to Amman at an annual rate of 50 to 95 million cubic metres, thereby causing irrigation water for the Valley to be below requirement at times.[128] A study in 2003 on the impact of water shortages on the cultivated area of the northern Jordan Valley concluded that cutting back irrigation water reduced cropping intensity, minimized cultivated area, reduced labour and lowered net income. Decreasing the water supply by 20 per cent reduced the cultivated area by about 14 per cent, leading to a net income decline of 15 per cent.[129] Moreover, a reduction in employment is accompanied by a direct and indirect loss in income, with significant implications for livelihoods and poverty levels of the Jordan Valley populations. Within the context of the latter, the poverty rate in the Jordan Valley is already significantly above the governorate average, at 32.2 per cent compared with 14.4 per cent in 2010.[130]

The Jordan Valley absorbs about 26 per cent of total agricultural labour, while irrigated areas employ more labour than rain-fed areas in

Jordan.[131] A study on the supporting capacity of water concluded that "for every unit flow of water diverted from rural Jordan Valley to urban areas with nothing returned for reuse, 160 families will be deprived of their means of livelihood and have to follow that water to urban areas".[132] With water already diverted to Amman, about 60 per cent of that water returns to the Jordan Valley. However, the loss of 40 per cent of the water originally allocated to the Jordan Valley has resulted in 2,880 families leaving the Valley for opportunities in Amman.[133] Rural-urban migration has drained off a steady stream of young men and sometimes entire families; agriculture as a way of life has declined alarmingly and local villages provide few employment opportunities for residents. Given the relatively low returns and incentives, a growing number of young people are unwilling to work in agriculture despite the availability of jobs at the family and community level. The increasing pull of youth to work in cities is resulting in a loss of labour force and growing food insecurity.[134]

The internal migration from rural to urban areas can be linked directly to agricultural activity. Land fragmentation affects food production and is a direct result of rapid population growth. Landholdings that are too small to provide adequate livelihoods are often turned into part-time farms, with some household members staying at home to tend crops while others (often the men) migrate in search of wage employment. Alternatively, land is sold to wealthier landowners, thereby making land distribution more uneven and adding to the creation of a large pool of landless labourers.[135]

In Jordan, while agriculture can be carried out over some 400,000 hectares, farming is practised on half of this potential area owing to the insecurity associated with erratic rainfall, among other reasons. Irrigated agriculture, however, provides most of the agricultural production in the country and accounts for a higher percentage of agricultural jobs and

other jobs in support services. Consequently, disruptions in irrigation services in the Jordan Valley greatly impacts food security for these vulnerable populations. Given the nature of the land and need for irrigation, many rural poor people cannot grow enough crops to feed themselves and their families during water shortages. While agriculture remains a critical livelihood source for farmers in rural areas, they have reduced their dependence on it, owing in part to chronic water shortages and fewer livestock holdings, stemming from the drop in fodder subsidies and deteriorating natural resources.[136] In terms of coping strategies, poor rural households often resort to using children as family labour when necessary rather than hire outside labour; poor women work in casual daily labour on large farms; and some households rely on domestic gardens to supplement consumption needs.

Many of Jordan's rural poor people live in extremely difficult conditions that increase their vulnerability to water scarcity. The salient issues are as follows:

- They have limited access to alternative sources of income;
- They have limited opportunities to diversify their farming enterprises as a result of low rainfall, poor soil quality and the topography of the land that they cultivate;
- They lack collateral and cannot obtain loans needed for investment in farm activities that could lead to higher incomes;
- They do not own land and are unwilling to make long-term investments on the land they cultivate as tenant farmers;
- They are often indebted to middlemen who market their products;
- In large families with unemployed adults and elderly parents, there is a high dependency ratio.

The landless farmers are even more vulnerable, given that they depend on wage labour engaged in informal employment as sharecroppers. They often have limited access to public services or credit, particularly given that credits often require collateral, and they rely on employers for additional assistance. Owing to social norms and inheritance structures, women-headed households tend to be landless: only 44 per cent of such households own land, compared to 68 per cent of male-headed households. A disproportionate percentage of women are landless due to socioeconomic constraints on land ownership. Moreover, women tend to have less access to credit (21 per cent), compared to men (43 per cent).[137] Women in these areas are traditionally responsible for the household economy and are active in fieldwork as well. Women make crucial contributions in agriculture and rural areas in farming, animal husbandry and as day labourers. While women are primarily responsible for providing water to households and contribute significantly to agricultural activities, they do not always possess decision-making authority on key water purchases, use, allocation or efficiency issues.[138]

Equally vulnerable are large families and families with very little land. These groups live in extreme poverty. Assets and access to support networks for the landless and women are limited, increasing their vulnerability to external shocks. During water shortages, wage labour is usually the first to be dropped in favour of increased reliance on family labour, thereby increasing their vulnerability to income, food and water insecurity. As water is the key input of production, its scarcity translates into reducing cultivation

---

**Box 9.** Reducing water rations impacting the viability of Abu Khalid's farm

Abu Khalid is a first-generation farmer who started working in agriculture in the 1980s, motivated by a national policy that promoted agricultural activity in the Jordan Valley. The area, which is known locally as al-Aghwar, consists of fertile lowlands with warm, year-round temperatures that suit the cultivation of a wide range of agricultural crops and vegetables. Finance and agricultural extension services were made available to famers such as Abu Khalid to maximize the agricultural yield, boosted by the King Abdullah Canal that supplies irrigation water from the Golan Heights and the Yarmouk River.

Agricultural activity seemed promising and Abu Khalid started to produce crops for the commercial market and also to supply milk, cheese, fresh vegetables and grapes for his own family. Khalid, the eldest son in the family, specialized in veterinarian medicine and intended to work on the farm and start a career in agribusiness and livestock. However, just before the turn of the century, their farm, as many others, started to face significant problems related to accessing sufficient quantities and suitable quality of water.

For example, in March 2009, Jordan had to shut down pumping from the King Abdullah Canal to farmlands in al-Aghwar for two days when contaminants were detected in the water. While this was a necessary step given that such a contamination could have increased salinity and negatively affected nutrients in soil, this represented a loss in water supply of 50,000 cubic metres. Such interruptions have taken their toll on farmers such as Abu Khalid, who suffer from income loss arising from reduced water rations and incur additional costs in order to cope with the resulting water shortages.

Furthermore, repeated heat waves, increasing and competing demands for water, as well as recurrent sudden intense weather changes have collectively resulted in multiple financial losses for Abu Khalid. Such incidents have affected various stages of the agricultural cycle, thereby resulting in the loss of produce and in wasted investments.

**Source:** Story based on interview communication with Abu Khalid's son, 9 June 2015.

---

and production. Subsequently, poor farmers have fewer products to sell and have less to eat. Hunger and food insecurity are constant threats. These populations are thus extremely vulnerable to disruptions in irrigation and/or price fluctuations in accessing water, pumping water or delivery of water.

Within the framework of its Poverty Reduction Strategy 2013-2020, Jordan emphasizes the strong linkage between agriculture, rural development and environment. The key policy and technical issues related to the design of pro-poor agriculture, environment and rural development include creating productive employment and income generation opportunities for the rural poor, especially small holders who need support in farming their land through microfinance and extension services; by developing agro-processing value chains aimed at creating new jobs; and by increasing local food production for consumption by rural residents and for food supplies to Jordan's urban populations.[139]

(d) Recommendations for overcoming vulnerability to water scarcity in the Jordan Valley

There is without doubt a critical need to reduce Jordan's overall water vulnerability by improving an integrated water resource management, and by identifying new and unconventional water resources, such as the Red-Dead Canal desalination project. However, measures that increase resilience of specific vulnerable populations to water scarcity also need urgent attention. Within the context of vulnerable groups, there is also a need to focus on population-specific issues, behaviours and education in order to increase resilience to water vulnerability. The following recommendations need to be considered to address the above-mentioned challenges:

(i) **Water reuse:** Treated wastewater for irrigation is the key intervention that has reduced water vulnerability in the agricultural sector. Specifically, wastewater

effluent added to water stock for use in irrigated agriculture can help to offset the significant imbalance in the population-water resources equation and could constitute a substantial percentage of irrigation water in future years.[140] A total of 98 per cent of treated wastewater is used by agriculture, mainly in the Jordan Valley, and treated water represents 61 per cent of irrigation water. Treated wastewater is being used on an increasing scale for irrigation, primarily in the Jordan Valley, and there are aims to increase treated wastewater to reach 280 million cubic metres by 2030.[141]

(ii) **Participatory water management:** Despite insufficient water levels, farmers in the Jordan Valley show remarkable cooperation. The Water User Associations (WUAs), which have gradually assumed responsibility of water management and distribution since 2001, have been able to distribute irrigation water fairly through the participation of farmers. Currently, these associations serve 80 per cent of irrigated lands;[142] and the number of participating farmers reached 4,207 in 2012, representing 44.3 per cent of the total number of farmers in the Jordan Valley.[143] However, WUAs vary in efficiency and capacity, and only a small number of women are members.

(iii) **Efficiencies in irrigation:** In the Jordan Valley, water transfer systems have been changed from open-channel systems to pressurized pipe systems, thereby reducing losses from evaporation. The adoption of drip irrigation systems has also greatly increased efficiency. Permaculture and enhanced agro-systems are effective alternatives, given that they reduce reliance on water, require less intensive investments in the agriculture and water sectors, and increase the unit value of revenue from the production. Community representatives who expressed their interest in the permaculture concept explained that such approaches could help to sustain their families without a need to depend on external sources for maintaining long-term farming viability, and stressed the importance of including women in these activities.

**(iv) Moving farmers into higher-value and less water-intensive crops:** As a general economic rule, a scarce resource, such as water in Jordan, should go to the sector which can maximize the economic return. However, water is also a human right and a sustainable development goal (access to safe drinking water and sanitation). It is often necessary to subsidize water use in order to meet basic societal needs, regardless of economic return. Nevertheless, water subsidies should be targeted to the underprivileged, with tariff rates better reflecting economic pricing.

In order to improve "crop per drop" returns on investment, capacity-building efforts aimed at improving linkages between researchers, policymakers and end users must also seek to connect market research on product demand with scientific and technological research on crop water needs and water dispersion possibilities. There is currently a mismatch between water intensity and efficiency with crop prices and returns on investment.[144] A study conducted in 2004 revealed that one cubic metre of water produced JD 0.57 ($0.80) of gross revenue.[145] Given that Jordan registers an actual average cost of JD 2 ($2.82) per cubic metre,[146] current agricultural crop choices are in fact drawing down subsidy budgets and do not make economic sense. For example, farmers growing such water-consuming crops as tomatoes should instead focus their production on crops that use less water and have higher economic value.

Incentives to encourage farmer behaviour change may also be needed. A study carried out by the Highland Water Forum indicated that farmers lack the technical and financial resources to shift from water-intensive

cultivations and inefficient irrigation systems to environmentally aware and economically feasible investments.[147] Subsidies for farming practices that result in negative water returns should be removed.

(e) Moving subsistence farmers into alternative livelihoods

As a result of rising water prices brought on by increasing water shortages and competing sectors, some stakeholders will be economically unable to continue to participate in the agricultural sector. Small farmers and subsistence farmers will be most affected by an increase in water tariffs and the high costs of new technologies that reduce water use on farms. The most vulnerable will be women and poor small and landless farmers. In general, increasing water scarcity and higher costs associated with water availability, distribution and extraction will have a large impact on the rural economy and will likely result in increased rural-to-urban migration and associated social problems. As such, considerations for policy change targeting these populations should involve building the capacity of small farmers to enter alternative and less water-intensive activities so that they can earn a livelihood instead of using limited resource for undependable agriculture.

(f) Linking energy vulnerability to water vulnerability

In Jordan, the energy costs of pumping water from groundwater aquifers for agricultural purposes represent 10 per cent of agricultural inputs,[148] while the water sector consumes 14 per cent of electricity produced in Jordan. Ongoing efforts to create new freshwater resources, such as the Red Dead Canal, will require increasingly high levels of energy resources, which will tie new water resources to increased energy needs. There is therefore a need to consider a variety of strategies that reduce population dependence and income vulnerability to both water and energy. These trends will require reassessing poverty alleviation strategies in order to focus both on population subgroups whose livelihoods are increasingly water and energy dependent, and on income vulnerability stemming from rising water and energy costs.

## 4. Mafraq

The sudden influxes of migrants and refugees over the past 60 years have exerted heavy pressure on natural resources, infrastructure, public services, housing and other services. Since 2011, the crisis in the Syrian Arab Republic has resulted in approximately 1.1 million refugees, including some 600,000 registered with UNHCR,[149] thereby representing an increase in the national population of least a 10 per cent. Overall, 33 per cent of the total number of Syrian refugees in Jordan have settled in Mafraq, resulting in an increase of 128 per cent in the Governorate population, and placing higher pressure on already stressed and dilapidated water and sanitation supplies and networks.[150] Al-Za'atari Camp, which was established 10 kilometres east of Mafraq in July 2012, accommodates 120,000 refugees and has become the second largest refugee camp in the world.[151] The vast majority of these arrivals is made up of destitute and women-headed households.

Moreover, given that trade with the Syrian Arab Republic and Iraq has contracted owing to the crisis, the people of Mafraq bear significant income vulnerability to water scarcity. The Governorate of Mafraq has the country's highest poverty rate, highest female illiteracy rate, highest population growth rate, and largest household size of all governorates, according to census data for 2004 by the Department of Statistics. The population of Mafraq is facing both extreme water stress and income vulnerability to water scarcity due to a variety of pre-existing socioeconomic factors that have been severely compounded by the sudden influx of refugees and the loss of trade-related livelihoods. The impact of this water stress has placed local populations at higher levels of risk with respect to social conflict, public health and food insecurity. Without a major infusion of new capital to develop these interventions, Jordan is expected to experience a serious degradation in services, increased levels of water-borne diseases and an inability of a large proportion of the population in the north – both Syrian and Jordanian – to lead productive lives. This is particularly important given that most experts fully anticipate the refugee presence to increase and remain a continuous concern over the next decade or even longer.

The impact of the Syrian influx is most acutely felt on the demand and provision of public services, where water and sanitation services are strained to the limit. Within the context of sudden population increase, large and impoverished families, Syrian and Jordanian alike, are especially vulnerable to water scarcity and shortages, with increasingly higher proportions of family income being allocated towards purchasing water.

### (a) Demographic and socioeconomic characteristics of Mafraq

The Governorate of Mafraq is situated in the north-east of the country and borders Iraq (east and north), the Syrian Arab Republic (north) and Saudi Arabia (south and east). It has an area of 26,552 km², amounting to 29.6 per cent of the total area of Jordan.[152] The Northern Badia (arid desert) region comprises the largest portion of the Governorate.

In 2011, the population was 293,700, with a per capita density of 9.5 per km².[153] The Governorate can be split into two main areas: Badia (rural) and urban areas. Urban areas house 40 per cent of Mafraq's population, mainly in the city of Mafraq.[154] Mafraq has always maintained a strategic position as it is situated at the crossroads of international routes linking Jordan to Iraq via the Karama entry point, as well as the Jaber border crossings into the Syrian Arab Republic, located 20 km from the Governorate's centre. The Syrian crisis has weighed heavily on the local urban trade, the bulk of which (around 80 per cent) was dependent on cross-border commercial activities.[155] In rural areas, agriculture forms a central element of the economy, especially in the more fertile Houran Plateau in the west, where fruit and vegetable farming (56,970 km$^2$) produce 102,000 tonnes of fruit (apples and peaches) and 15,540 tonnes of vegetables (cabbages, onions, garlic and lettuce).[156] Eastern Jordan, which encompasses most of eastern Mafraq, is arid and uncultivable. The segment of rural population is spread over arid, desert regions with large tracts of land devoid of any water bodies, and often at high water stress levels.

As mentioned above, Jordan has absorbed some 1.1 million Syrians, all of them additional water users and with 80 per cent living in host communities. In terms of Syrian refugees in Jordan, 60 per cent are in the northern governorates and 33 per cent reside in Mafraq (figure 12).[157] Once home to 70,000-90,000 people, the city of Mafraq now has to cope with an additional 90,000 refugees and, as a result, water deficits have quadrupled. The percentage of Syrians to Jordanians exceeds 2 to 1 in 2013.[158] At the family level, the Jordan Hashemite Charity Organization and official data indicate that Syrian refugees are distributed in families composed of 5.8 persons per family. Statistics also show that women and children below the age of 11 make up 70 per cent of Syrian refugees.[159] Jordanian households in Mafraq on average have 5.9 members, with an average fertility rate of 4.1, both of which are among the highest averages in the country.[160] Approximately 41 per cent of the Jordanian population of Mafraq is under the age of 15, while more than 56 per cent is aged between 15 and 64; and 13.3 per cent of the population of Mafraq is illiterate.[161] The new combined Syrian-Jordanian population of Mafraq is therefore characterized by a youth bulge, comprising large households with low income levels.

Mafraq has the highest poverty rate of all governorates in Jordan, with 31.9 per cent of the population living below the poverty line.[162] Out of 32 poverty pockets (subdistricts with poverty rates that exceed 25 per cent), 10 are located in the Governorate of Mafraq.[163] Additionally, it has among the lowest national levels and rates of maternal and child health mortality, Gender Development Index, adult literacy, income and gross school enrolments.

On average, household income in Mafraq is an estimated JD 7,276 ($10,255), amounting to a per capita income little over JD 1,200 ($1,700) per annum;[164] and 11.9 per cent of households receive assistance from the National Aid Fund.[165] In those governorates most directly affected by the Syrian influx, the assets of poor households can be broken down as follows: structures used for family housing (71.2 per cent); land holdings (10.3 per cent); ownership of livestock (13.4 per cent); ownership of property for rental (3.1 per cent); and productive tools and other equipment (less than 2 per cent).[166] These assets significantly limit the capacity of vulnerable households in host communities to generate additional income, expand productivity or explore new livelihood strategies on their own in order to mitigate the impact of the Syrian crisis on their socioeconomic well-being.

The Syrian crisis has adversely impacted the population of Mafraq primarily in two ways:

(i) Border communities in Irbid and Mafraq that had benefitted from seeds, fertilizers and other materials subsidized by the Government of the Syrian Arab Republic, or had earned income by trading or smuggling Syrian agricultural materials through informal trade networks have lost livelihoods and have seen production costs rise significantly after the outbreak of the crisis;[167]

(ii) Overall, 33 per cent of the total number of Syrian refugees in Jordan have settled in Mafraq, suddenly increasing the population

**Figure 12.** Concentration of Syrians in Jordan, 2013

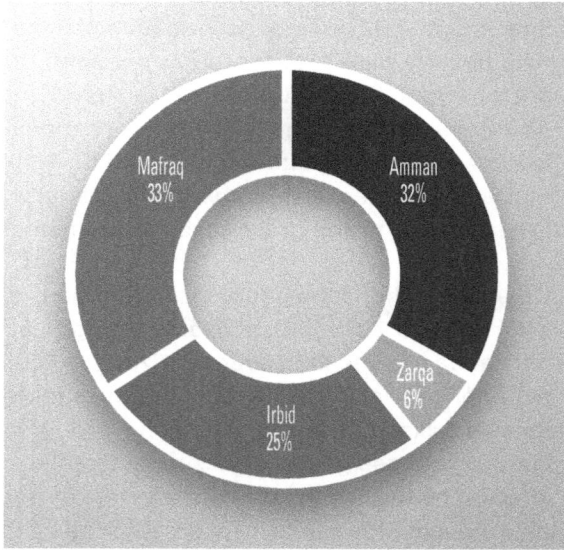

**Source:** Jordan, Ministry of Water and Irrigation and Ministry of Planning and International Cooperation, *Report of the High-level Conference on Jordan's Water Crisis*, Amman, 2 December 2013.

of Mafraq by 128 per cent, placing increased pressure on already stressed and dilapidated water and sanitation supplies and networks.[168] A high rate of natural population growth, combined with massive influxes of refugees, has created an imbalance between population and water.

Mafraq's municipalities rely on the country's treasury and have been unprepared to address such pressures that have strained the infrastructure and public services, including health, education, transport, garbage management, sanitation, water and power. The Syrian and Jordanian populations residing in the city of Mafraq face increasing water stress, which poses threats to food security, health and hygiene, and contributes to interethnic social conflict. The food security status of the poorest segments of society will be further impacted by the current upward pressure on rental prices, increased dependence on potable water from private vendors and potential price increases in other necessities, in addition to the loss of livelihoods in agriculture and trade, and increased competition for employment.[169]

(b) Water challenges and institutional framework in Mafraq

Mafraq, which is home to two groundwater basins, namely, the Azraq and the Hammad, sees most of the water of the Azraq being extracted for the cities of Amman and Zarqa. There are no water structures in Mafraq, such as dams, which could help to ensure water recharge. Data on water consumption in Mafraq can be divided into two main categories: household consumption, with 85.8 per cent of billed water use; and governmental use, with 8.2 per cent of billed water use.[170] Agricultural activities are largely supported by rain and irrigation drawn from well waters at low or no cost, and are often not recorded. Highland agriculture relies heavily on groundwater, thereby contributing to groundwater overabstraction, which is unsustainable. Abstraction remains considerably beyond safe yield. Industrial and commercial activities are limited; and water losses in Mafraq (78 per cent) are the highest in the country.[171] Water losses can be attributed to a lack of law enforcement, very low penalties for use of illegal water, a lack of individual responsibility or awareness for water wastage among citizens, low maintenance of the pipes, and poor quality of pipe repair materials.[172] Losses are either physical (poor networks, leaks and breakages) or administrative (theft, illegal use, metre bypassing and illegal pumping). An estimated 43 per cent of households in northern governorates are connected to sewage,[173] while in the Governorate of Mafraq only 8 per cent of households are connected.[174] There is one wastewater treatment plant in Mafraq, but this plant has experienced many technical difficulties and its performance is impaired.[175]

After the success of irrigation in the Jordan Valley, the Government promoted highland agriculture in the Northern Badia to encourage rural development. Expansion of farming in the highlands led farmers to pump more and more water from underground aquifers through WAJ-issued drilling licences. While the licences specified limits on groundwater abstraction, these were never enforced. The failure of WAJ to enforce these limits or to impose fines on violators led to a further rush of private land buying throughout the 1980s. Hundreds more wells were drilled in the highlands, putting increasing pressure on the crucial Amman-Zarqa and Azraq aquifers.[176]

Water is supplied to Mafraq and the northern governorates by the Yarmouk Water Company. Quantities of water consumed is categorized into "blocks" and billed per month. The lowest blocks (0-20 and 21-38 cubic metres) are subsidized for the poor, while the following blocks are priced at progressively increasing rates. Tariffs are set by the Government and are below the cost for full-cost recovery. All water resources in the northern governorates covered by the Yarmouk Water Company are currently at full capacity, pumping every day of the year with no seasonal modulation. Moreover, the rapid rise in the number of Syrian refugees caused a severe stress on public water supply systems, serving twice as many people than originally served in certain areas.[177] Prior to the influx, water was distributed at the household level once every week to two weeks for a maximum of six hours.

Emblematic of this situation is the Sumaya pump station, which sits on the frontline of the refugee crisis. Once serving around 80,000 people, it currently has to distribute water to more than 200,000.[178] The deficit is being met through overabstraction of groundwater aquifers. Once current basins have been depleted by 70 or 80 per cent, the water will no longer be drinkable. Indeed, the rate of exhaustion has likely accelerated since the onset of the refugee crisis. The increased load and limited capacity has resulted in a decrease in sanitation efficiency in Mafraq by 51.6 per cent.[179]

Mafraq's municipalities rely on the country's treasury and hence are unable to absorb the additional burdens imposed by the Syrian refugees. Already a water-scarce country, Jordan's water resources and services were overstretched even before the arrival of Syrian refugees. Massive water loss through system inefficiencies and population increase are straining the overall supply sources, especially in the northern areas of Jordan where demand for water services is increasing every day. Results also show that Jordan's 12 groundwater basins are overexploited, and the current model of water withdrawal is dangerously unsustainable. The overall water deficit in Jordan has sharply risen with the influx of Syrians. Of those most-affected governorates, a severe increase in deficit is noted in the Mafraq and Irbid Governorates, when examined under the normal conditions and the post-crisis scenarios. This dramatic population increase has impacted Jordan's water and sanitization sectors, and represents a significant strain on both the national economy and resources. Jordan estimates that water, sanitation and hygiene needs in areas affected by refugees amount to $930 million.[180]

(c) Impact of water scarcity on the populations of Mafraq

(i) Higher costs of water
The majority of households in Jordan pay less than JD 2 ($2.82) for piped water per month, and water tariffs for agriculture are even far lower (20-30 cents per cubic metre).[181] Among domestic, irrigation and industrial tariffs, the domestic tariff per capita is the highest in Jordan. The domestic (drinking) water pricing has considerable impact, particularly on the urban populations of Mafraq and on low-income groups. Metering consumption is not widespread; where it is present, it is shared by poor families, which are typically large in size. An average of 20 per cent of Jordanian households

share meters.[182] Among Syrians, it is not uncommon to see several Syrian families living together in homes composed of several wage earners, so that they share the burden of high rent and water and electricity bills. Poor households, whether Syrian or Jordanian, tend to be larger in size, and tend to share their meters with similar households, which results in higher consumption readings.

## (ii) Water rationing

In an effort to manage limited water resources, almost all urban domestic water is supplied on an intermittent and rationed basis. Prior to the influx in Mafraq, water was delivered once a week or fortnight for a maximum of six hours, and families relied on storage tanks or containers within the household to store water until the next supply. As a result of the influx, water is now distributed infrequently (once a week for a few hours), by rotation and by neighbourhood. Supply is disrupted by frequent water shortages and by weak water pressure, thereby requiring pumps to be installed at an extra cost to poor households along with the related electricity costs of running those pumps.

Intermittent flows also aggravate network problems with pressure shocks and damage to gauges, which in turn increase the danger of deteriorated network pipes sucking in sewage, with concomitant health risks.[183] Moreover, intermittent supply contributes to reduced water quality owing to poor storage facilities and stagnating water. Often, city dwellers do not invest in proper water practices, such as cleaning water tanks, or ensuring water storage tanks are located away from such contaminants as cesspits. There is little awareness of how water quality can change within the household system or the impact poor sanitary habits have on its deterioration. According to the WAJ laboratory director,

60-70 per cent of complaints relating to peculiar water taste or smell are caused by badly maintained roof tanks.[184] These factors place the community at increased risk of water borne diseases and reduced access to safe drinking water.

## (iii) Waste disposal

Sanitation services need to expand to handle the increase in waste generated: an estimated 340 tonnes of waste needs to be removed daily in the Mafraq municipality.[185] Municipal garbage collection is unable to keep up. Pollution, infestation of insects, rodents and stray dogs are a challenge.[186] Owing to the relatively low number of houses with sewage connectivity, waste disposal of sewage is also becoming problematic with increasing volumes. In Mafraq, 68 per cent of schools have septic tanks that are in poor condition, while 16 per cent of schools have no internal sewage networks.[187] Discharge of wastewater to a cesspool is the main common sanitation practice among households and is considered one of main threats that might contaminate groundwater resources. Dumping raw and partially treated wastewater from agriculture, industry and municipalities into water courses has caused grave health concerns and has severely polluted agricultural lands and water resources, especially during low discharge periods. The contamination of the underlying aquifers is also evident.[188] While studies have not yet been undertaken on the impact of poor waste management on public health, it is clear that the lack of solid waste disposal constitutes a health risk to urban dwellers from the potential contamination of the water supply through groundwater, stored water and environmental illnesses.

## (iv) Public health

The increasingly unhealthy water and sanitation conditions impact health, particularly the incidence of diarrhoea. A survey conducted in March 2013 on Syrian refugees in northern governorates revealed that the prevalence of diarrhoea in children aged under 2 was 7.2 per cent in Mafraq, higher than in other governorates surveyed.[189] Most diarrhoeal cases can be attributed to a lack of improved water and sanitation. This is reminiscent of an incident in Mafraq in 2009 when people reported that their tap water had turned yellow and experts confirmed that the water had been contaminated by sewage. In 2009, nearly 1,000 people from a village near the city of Mafraq developed diarrhoea and high fever from cryptosporidium, a parasite that had made its way into the local water system. Investigations revealed that the disease had spread as a result of the city's dilapidated water network.[190] The current state of Mafraq's already derelict water network makes water supply more susceptible to contamination due to the combined threats of disruption, namely, rationing and increasing discharge of wastewater into unmanaged cesspools.

### (v) Social conflict

In the northern governorates, particularly in Mafraq, water scarcity is closely linked to social tensions and conflict. These tensions stem from the low level of development, increased costs of living and competition for housing and jobs. Water shortages and improper management are seen as cause for unrest.[191] Specifically, public opinion on Syrian refugees revolves around wasteful water use, and water shortages are blamed on Syrians. In total, 30 per cent of respondents of the REACH Initiative survey in 2014 cited water shortages as a driver of tension in accessing water in the community. Female respondents most commonly cited water shortages as causing tension in their community (32 per cent), while

the cause for tension most commonly cited by male respondents was uneven access to water between Jordanians and Syrians (31 per cent).[192] Within that context, poor households with large numbers of dependants and children, and women-headed households are especially vulnerable to water scarcity.

As competition for scarce resources increases, social conflict between Syrians and Jordanians are set to rise over both scarce water resources and livelihood opportunities. Poor water management has led to water scarcity, which intensifies the struggle to gain access to and control the resource, thereby resulting in discrimination and violence. Given the severe water rationing, particularly in urban areas such as Mafraq whose populations have doubled, residents must rely on water delivered by private tanker companies, which is a costly alternative that fuels further resentment against the influx of Syrians.[193] This conflict is likely to be most pronounced among poorer families living under or near the poverty line. Already children in schools have preconceived ideas about the "other" residing within their communities. In Jordan, and especially in the northern governorates, water scarcity has therefore become a threat to national security, social well-being and political stability.[194] Exploring ways in which communal solutions for the protection and sustainable use of common resources will be critical.

### (vi) Income vulnerability

Families in urban Mafraq, whether Syrian or Jordanian, sharing housing as a coping mechanism for poverty, usually end up in the higher water tariff blocks despite their modest per capita use of water. As a result, they spend a larger proportion of their income on purchasing municipal water than households with smaller sizes who do not share their meters. The proportion of income allotted to buying domestic/drinking water in water-scarce Mafraq is 6.9 per cent.[195] However, some communities often pay private contractors and end up spending up to one third of their income on water, especially if they are buying tanker water.[196] When families experience water shortages owing to rationing, they purchase water from water tankers at three or four times the price of municipal water.[197] According to the Yarmouk Water Company that supplies the northern governorates, this water deficit is estimated at 16 litres per person per day. This is in the range of the volume purchased from private tankers by the majority of respondents, whether Jordanian or Syrian, to compensate for water shortages, particularly during summer. Overall, monthly expenditure on water for drinking and other uses varies between JD 15 and JD 80 ($21 and $113).[198] Given that monthly household income in Mafraq is an average of JD 600 (approximately $846), water purchase can amount to 13 per cent of income. Additionally, emptying septic tanks is expensive, and prices have risen from JD 25 to JD 30 ($35 to $42) owing to demand, thereby prompting some house owners to dispose of effluent illegally. The prices for emptying septic tanks and those charged by private water tankers are not regulated by the Government. This is a situation that puts an unjustified burden on lower-income families who have no other choice.[199]

*(vii) Food insecurity among poor, large households and women*

Among poor, large households of Mafraq, the largest proportion of household expenditure is devoted to food. Even families that receive food vouchers are compelled to purchase additional food, sometimes on credit. In the northern governorates of Jordan, it has been found that people increasingly resort to negative coping mechanisms, such as selling personal items or buying food and essential items on credit, thereby contributing to household debt. As water costs increase, particularly as a function of purchased water and pumping costs, household debt accordingly rises along with vulnerability to food insecurity. This impacts Syrian and Jordanian households alike. In July 2014, the World Food Programme assessed that those Syrian households with limited income or unskilled jobs were most vulnerable to food insecurity, and that widowed heads of household were far more likely to be food insecure than most other static variables.

A recent study on the prevalence of food insecurity among women in Irbid linked food insecurity risk directly to water scarcity, among other factors.[200] According to the study, approximately one third of women in northern Jordan are food insecure, where such factors as low levels of education, poverty and unemployment increased the probability of food insecurity. This vulnerability is more pronounced where women are not connected to the public water supply. The increased expense

"Not having water adds a lot of pressure to people", said Um Omar, a single mother living in northern Jordan. Sometimes she would go to neighbours to ask for water, but often they were nearly as desperate. "I was worried all the time. It is a major source of anxiety. A woman having to go to her neighbours in the middle of the night" – she waved her hand – "she feels her dignity taken away".

**Source**: Mercy Corps, "Water scarcity and the Syrian refugee crisis", 9 March 2014. Available from www.mercycorps.org.uk/articles/jordan/water-scarcity-and-syrian-refugee-crisis.

of water for poor households is linked to rising vulnerability to food insecurity.

*(viii) Impact on women*

In their homes, women are most often the collectors, users and managers of water. At the household level, women and children are usually responsible for carrying out water-related activities inside the house as well as gardening.[201] This is even more evident in poor households, where women devote a sizeable portion of their days to such water-related activities as storing water, cleaning and laundry. In households, women often purchase drinking water or boil tap water in order to keep their family members healthy. This role as manager of household water places a large responsibility on women to manage this resource, albeit with limited voice in household infrastructure decisions. In their role as water managers, women across Jordan engage in household chores and laundry on water day, reuse water (such as bathing children in same water) and regulate bathing frequency. In their roles as caregivers, women are also the most likely to be susceptible to impacts on health, hygiene and nutrition stemming from water scarcity. Within that context of increased vulnerability arising from water-borne diseases, women have less access to medical services than men, and their workloads increase when they have to spend more time caring for the sick. An increase in water-borne disease outbreaks will have significantly different impacts on women than on men.

(d) Recommendations for overcoming vulnerability to water scarcity in Mafraq

*(i) Rainwater harvesting*

Prior to the influx of Syrian refugees, communities in the north had begun to embark on community-based initiatives that would reduce their water vulnerability, with the most notable being rainwater

harvesting. Given the greater precipitation in northern Jordan than in the rest of the country, much of the rainwater harvesting programming has occurred in the northern governorates. Mercy Corps, which is currently implementing the USAID-Community Based Initiatives for Water Demand Management Project, has instituted community-based programming through revolving loans aimed at installing rainwater harvesting equipment, tools and systems. The loans enable community members – households, farms and such communal facilities as schools and mosques – to install rainwater harvesting, preserve ancient wells, maintain residential networks, install drip irrigation systems, and maintain irrigation channels and water springs. This reduces dependence on purchased water and serves households and farms that are not connected to networks, thereby boosting resilience to water vulnerability. To date, the project has enabled community members to harvest 810,000 cubic metres of water.[202]

*(ii) Water filtration*

Reverse osmosis units can help to improve water quality in households. Given the current and previous water crises, small and medium units have spread in the market, with vendors currently selling or distributing treated water on demand. In Amman alone, more than 120 small businesses are in operation. Many households have installed small reverse osmosis units to ensure adequate drinking water quality.[203] However, the coverage of reverse osmosis units is still limited, particularly in low-income households in the north of the country.

*(iii) National Resilience Plan (2014-2016)*

At the national level, the Ministry of Planning and International Cooperation, in collaboration with the Ministry of Water and Irrigation and the international donor community, has developed the three-year National Resilience Plan (2014-2016) aimed at responding to the impact of the Syrian influx on the social, livelihood, municipal, water and sanitation sectors of the host populations, particularly in the northern governorates. The Plan lays out in detail the support needed to help bolster resilience in Irbid and Mafraq. Within that context, the Plan allocates $930 million of investment in water and sanitation, and municipal waste disposal for northern governorates. To date, work on rehabilitating the water conveyance system has been implemented, but new waste treatment facilities are still needed.

(iv) *Reallocating water resources for increased water productivity*
Growing water shortages increase demand for basic needs of water and, at the same time, reduce the amount of water available for agricultural purposes. This is particularly relevant in the agricultural sector where reducing the production of highly water-intensive crops can reduce water vulnerability. This can be accomplished by moving to more economically viable crops. In addition, for food security, Jordan needs to explore the possibility of trade in "virtual water" by importing high water-consuming crops from countries that are more water-endowed.

(v) *Reducing non-revenue and water inefficiency at the household level*
There is an obvious need for more efficient and effective water policies, metering of water use and collection of water tariffs, especially where non-revenue water is high. In urban areas in particular, installing universal water metering is an essential element in conserving water because it leads to a change in behaviour by allowing customers to track their consumption and thereby reduce water use. Education of

positive water behaviours through water audits within the household can promote improved water quality and water conservation. Retrofitting through rebate programmes have provided incentives to customers in countries, such as Canada, to invest in efficient household appliances (for example, washing machines and toilets) and have helped to save water and energy.[204]

(vi) *Reducing the economic burden on the poorest households*
While water tariffs are affordable to the general population, marginalized and water-vulnerable population groups, especially those falling under the poverty line, allocate a significant portion of their income to water, whether as a result of purchasing water from tanker trucks, paying to empty septic tanks, or falling into higher tariff blocks owing to meter sharing. This situation puts an additional economic burden on lower-income families, resulting in severe income vulnerability to water scarcity. There is a need to take a holistic approach that links basic water and sanitation requirements to comprehensive development strategies that can ensure human rights to water and sanitation for these vulnerable populations.

(e) Recommendations for overcoming vulnerability to water scarcity in Mafraq and the Jordan Valley

(i) *Gender and water*
In both case studies in Jordan, women, especially women-headed households, emerge as vulnerable population groups. While there is no perceived discrimination in water provision between men and women, the different gender roles with respect to accessing water and water use, management and decision-making can cause increased water vulnerability for women. This is particularly true for women in agriculture and those women-headed households that lack assets (land) and

access. Within the household, women are charged with managing water, caring for the sick and household hygiene. As such, water scarcity impacts women differently. There is a need to draw attention to gender differentials with respect to water use in order to better determine water vulnerability and enhance resilience.

(ii) *Water vulnerability – adaptive capacity index*
The Royal Society for the Conservation of Nature has recently started to assess the adaptive capacities of local communities around protected areas regarding the impacts of climate change. Globally, adaptive capacity to climate change indices take into account the following factors: economic resources, technology, information skills and management, infrastructure, institutions and networks, and equity.[205] These indices are able to capture the adaptive capacity of differing population groups based on various characteristics as well as sector or regional contexts. Such an indicator could also be modified to assess adaptive capacity to water vulnerability in order to identify both key population subgroups that are experiencing high levels of vulnerability to water scarcity, and to pinpoint socioeconomic, infrastructural, institutional, technological and educational fault lines pertaining to vulnerable groups. Such an indicator could better inform policymakers, thereby allowing them to assess the water vulnerability of increasingly exposed groups and improve targeted programming.

(iii) *Education*
Efforts are currently underway aimed at building resilience of local communities in Jordan, including municipal capacity-building, local economic development, community-based rainwater harvesting, repair of water conveyancing systems and sanitation facilities. However, there is still significant work that remains to be done in terms of educating people on water quality and hygiene in order to reduce their health vulnerability, and retrofitting households to improve water efficiency and reduce non-revenue water.

# Conclusion

"Accelerating global progress on water and sanitation under the new SDG agenda is possible. It will require all of us working together, and a lot of innovation and ambition."

*Helen Clark, Administrator of UNDP*

# IV. Conclusion

One can hardly think of a natural resource that is more vital for human life than water. Water is also indispensable for the economic and social development of countries and, therefore, for people's well-being.

As demonstrated throughout this report, the linkages between water scarcity and population issues are apparent and manifest through a number of development areas, including health, education, poverty elevation and food security. For example, water plays an important role as an economic good needed to maintain complex freshwater ecosystems that provide economically valuable results, such as habitat for plants and animals, sustainable fishing, transportation channels, and purification of human and industrial wastes.[1] The issue of water scarcity has to be addressed in an integrated fashion within a sustainable development framework aimed at advancing the well-being of people through the promotion of economic and social development, in a way that does not compromise the environment.

This nexus makes water scarcity a multidimensional issue and puts emphasis on addressing it in a holistic and integrated manner, with due consideration to local specificities and population needs. Recommendations drawn in the three different case studies in chapter III are not intended to be universal; this report does not seek to provide a set of universally applicable recommendations or "one-size-fits-all" solutions. Rather, it endeavours to show that the impact of water scarcity varies between population groups, thereby making a case for a people-centred policy approach that can address the specific needs of specific populations and sociodemographic groups. This is vital both at the local level and, with regard to future development agendas, at national and global levels.

Subsequent to the Millennium Development Goals, the 2030 Agenda for Sustainable Development is a cross-thematic agenda that offers a unique opportunity to approach the issue of water scarcity in an integrated way. The framework argues for an overarching and holistic approach for addressing development issues, including challenges linked to water availability and management. Goal 6 contains a number of targets around improving access to safe drinking water, improving sanitation and hygiene and increasing water-use efficiency.[2]

This report shows that the poorest and marginalized communities are often the first to lose out when there is competition over scarce water resources. Yet these groups are rarely considered in the formulation of policies and are seldom given any voice in decision-making processes that address such issues as access to safe drinking water, water management and sustainable use of water resources.

The proposed new development framework makes it explicit that all 17 proposed sustainable development goals are interdependent and mutually reinforcing. Only integrated strategies addressing water resource issues can reconcile the needs of different users – large and small populations, rural and urban, male and female, and young and old – for energy, food production and creation of livelihoods, while ensuring that ecosystems are preserved for posterity. This approach promulgated by the new set of goals aims to achieve fair, balanced and sustainable water use going forward that is beneficial to all segments of population, including the poorest, most vulnerable and most marginalized.

Governments of Arab countries must become aware of the critical role that local communities play in water resource management and climate change adaptation, and recognize that only an integrated and comprehensive model, fully cognizant of population issues, can be the common sense and logical solution to water scarcity impact on population in the Arab region.

# Endnotes

**Introduction**

1. The Arab region consists of all 22 member countries of the League of Arab States, namely: Algeria, Bahrain, Comoros, Djibouti, Egypt, Iraq, Jordan, Kuwait, Lebanon, Libya, Mauritania, Morocco, Oman, Palestine, Qatar, Saudi Arabia, Somalia, Sudan, Syrian Arab Republic, Tunisia, United Arab Emirates and Yemen.
2. United Nations Environment Programme (UNEP), *Arab Region: Atlas of our Changing Environment* (2013). Available from http://na.unep.net/atlas/viewAtlasBookWithID.php?atlasID=2447.
3. United Nations Environment Programme (UNEP), Economic and Social Commission for Western Asia (ESCWA) and League of Arab States, "Air quality and atmospheric pollution in the Arab region" (2006). Available from www.un.org/esa/sustdev/csd/csd14/escwaRIM_bp1.pdf.
4. UNEP, *Arab Region: Atlas.*
5. United Nations Educational, Scientific and Cultural Organization (UNESCO), *World Water Development Report III: Water in a Changing World* (2009), p. 29. Available from www.unesco.org/new/en/natural-sciences/environment/water/wwap/wwdr/wwdr3-2009/.

**Chapter I**

1. See Population Action International, "Why population matters to water resources" (2011), p. 2; and F. Roudi-Fahimi, L. Creel and R. M. De Souza, *Finding the Balance: Population and Water Scarcity in the Middle East and North Africa*, MENA Policy Brief (Washington, D.C., Population Reference Bureau, 2002).
2. J. Devlin, "Is water scarcity dampening growth prospects in the Middle East and North Africa?", 24 June 2014. Available from www.brookings.edu/research/opinions/2014/06/24-water-scarcity-growth-prospects-middle-east-north-africa-devlin.
3. A. Zyadin, "Water shortage in MENA region: An interdisciplinary overview and a suite of practical solutions", *Journal of Water Resource and Protection*, vol. 5 (2013), pp. 49-58. Available from http://dx.doi.org/10.4236/jwarp.2013.54A008.
4. Groundwater Governance – A Global Framework for Action, "Regional diagnostic

report: Arab States region". Available from www.groundwatergovernance.org/.
5. UNDP, *Water Governance in the Arab Region.*
6. Ibid.
7. Ibid.
8. ESCWA, Arab Countries Water Utilities Association (ACWUA) and League of Arab States, "First report of the MDG+ Initiative" (2015).
9. UNDP, *Water Governance in the Arab Region.*
10. ESCWA, ACWUA and League of Arab States, "First report of the MDG+ Initiative".
11. Beyond 2015 Campaign, "Population dynamics in the context of the post-2015 development agenda" (2013), p. 4.
12. Ibid.
13. Technical Support Team, "TST Issues Brief: Population dynamics" (2014), p. 1.
14. United Nations, "The future we want: Outcome document adopted at Rio+20" (2012).
15. United Nations Population Fund (UNFPA) and others, *Population Dynamics in the Post-2015 Development Agenda: Report of the Global Thematic Consultation on Population Dynamics* (2013).
16. Technical Support Team, "Population dynamics", p. 2.
17. Beyond 2015 Campaign, "Population dynamics".
18. Technical Support Team, "Population dynamics".
19. ESCWA calculations are based on data provided in United Nations, Department of Economic and Social Affairs, *World Population Prospects: The 2012 Revision* (United Nations, 2014).
20. Water-stress countries are defined as those States that are below 1,000 cubic metres of renewable freshwater per capita per year. UNESCO, *World Water Development Report III.*
21. Roudi-Fahimi, Creel and de Souza R., *Finding the Balance.*
22. Population Action International, "Why population matters", p. 2.
23. Ibid.
24. Ibid.
25. Roudi-Fahimi, Creel and de Souza R., *Finding the Balance.*
26. Population Action International, "Why population matters".

27. Roudi-Fahimi, Creel and de Souza R., *Finding the Balance.*
28. Ibid.
29. ESCWA, *The Demographic Profile of the Arab Countries* (2013).
30. UNFPA and others, *Population Dynamics.*
31. Ibid., p. 13.
32. UNESCO, *World Water Development Report III*, p. 31.
33. Population Action International, "Why population matters".
34. United Nations Department of Economic and Social Affairs, *World Urbanization Prospects: The 2014 Revision* (United Nations, 2014).
35. Population Action International, "Why population matters".
36. UNFPA and others, *Population Dynamics.*
37. R. Jedwab, L. Christiaensen and M. Gindelsky, *Demography, Urbanization and Development: Rural Push, Urban Pull and... Urban Push?* (Washington, D.C., World Bank, 2015).
38. United Nations, "The future we want", p. 26.
39. Technical Support Team, "Population dynamics".
40. UNFPA and others, *Population Dynamics.*
41. Technical Support Team, "Population dynamics".
42. UNFPA and others, *Population Dynamics*, p. 13.
43. Ibid.
44. UNESCO, *World Water Development Report III*, p. 30.
45. Ibid.
46. Roudi-Fahimi, Creel and de Souza R., *Finding the Balance.*
47. UNDP, *Water Governance in the Arab Region.*
48. Population Action International, "Why population matters", p. 2.
49. UNDP, *Water Governance in the Arab Region*, p. 2.
50. Roudi-Fahimi, Creel and de Souza R., *Finding the Balance.*
51. UNESCO, *World Water Development Report III.*
52. United Nations, Department of Economic and Social Affairs, *World Urbanization Prospects: The 2014 Revision.*
53. United Nations High Commissioner for Refugees (UNHCR), Syria Regional Refugee Response: Inter-agency Information Sharing Portal. Available from http://data.unhcr.org/

syrianrefugees/regional.php#_ga=1.2729
0108.1569209750.1391411725 (accessed 19
February 2015).

54. Ibid.

55. UNESCO, *World Water Development Report III*.

56. Internal Displacement Monitoring Centre (IDMC), Global figures. Available from www. internal-displacement.org/global-figures (accessed 19 February 2015).

57. Technical Support Team, "Population dynamics", p. 5.

58. Beyond 2015 Campaign, "Population dynamics".

59. United Nations Human Settlements Programme (UN-Habitat), *The State of Arab Cities 2012: Challenges of Urban Transition*, Second edition (2012), p. viii.

Chapter II

1. UNFPA and others, *Population Dynamics*.

2. Population Action International, "Why population matters".

3. K. Thywissen, *Components of Risk: A Comparative Glossary* (Bonn, United Nations University, Institute for Environment and Human Security, 2006).

4. The glossary of terms related to the components of risk, which is supported by the United Nations University Institute for Environment and Human Security, highlights the problems stemming from the existence and interchangeable use of a wide range of definitions for each term.

5. W.C. Clark and others, *Assessing Vulnerability to Global Environmental Risks*, ENRP Discussion Paper 2000-12 (Belfer Center for Science and International Affairs, John F. Kennedy School of Government, Harvard University, 2000).

6. S. Schneiderbauer and D. Ehrlich, *Risk, Hazard and People's Vulnerability to Natural Hazards. A Review of Definitions, Concepts and Data* (Luxembourg, Office for Official Publication of the European Communities, 2004).

7. P. McLaughlin and T. Dietz, "Structure, agency and environment: Toward an integrated perspective on vulnerability", *Global Environmental Change*, vol. 18, No. 1 (Elsevier, 2008), pp. 99-111.

8. See S. L. Cutter, B. Boruff and W. L. Shirley, "Social vulnerability to environmental hazards", *Social Science Quarterly*, vol. 84, No. 2 (2003), pp. 242-261; W. N. Adger, "Vulnerability", *Global Environmental Change*, vol. 16, No. 3 (2006); pp. 268-281; and McLaughlin and Dietz, "Structure, agency and environment".

9. I. Alcantara-ayala, "Geomorphology, natural hazards, vulnerability and prevention of natural disasters in developing countries", *Geomorphology*, vol. 47, Nos. 2-4 (2002), pp. 107-124.

10. J. Dayton-Johnson, "Natural disasters and adaptive capacity", OECD Development Centre, Working Paper No. 237 (2004).

11. N. Brooks, W.N. Adger and P.M. Kelly, "The determinants of vulnerability and adaptive capacity at the national level and the implications for adaptation", *Global Environmental Change*, vol. 15, No. 2 (2005).

12. Thywissen, *Components of Risk*.

13. "There is a personal or individual potential for, or sensitivity to, losses (or harm) that have both spatial and non spatial domains. This is termed individual vulnerability. Social vulnerability includes the susceptibility of social groups or society at large to potential losses (structural and non structural) from hazard events and disasters". S.L. Cutter, "Vulnerability to environmental hazards", *Progress in Human Geography*, vol. 20, No. 4 (1996), pp. 529-539.

14. Ibid.

15. McLaughlin and Dietz, "Structure, agency and environment".

16. See, for example, Cutter, "Vulnerability to environmental hazards"; and Clark and others, *Assessing Vulnerability*.

17. Cutter, "Vulnerability to environmental hazards".

18. Intergovernmental Panel on Climate Change (IPCC), *Climate Change 2001: Impacts, Adaptation and Vulnerability – Contribution of Working Group II to the Third Assessment Report of the Intergovernmental Panel on Climate Change* (Cambridge, Cambridge University Press, 2001), chap. 18. Available from www.ipcc.ch/ipccreports/tar/wg2/index.php?idp=0.

19. Clark and others, *Assessing Vulnerability*.

20. Adger, "Vulnerability".

21. See Cutter, "Vulnerability to environmental hazards"; and B. L. Turner and others, "A framework for vulnerability analysis in sustainability science", *Proceedings of the National Academy of Sciences of the United States of America*, vol. 100, No. 14 (2003), pp. 8074-8079.

22. Brooks, Adger and Kelly, "The determinants of vulnerability".

23. Turner and others, "A framework for vulnerability analysis".

24. McLaughlin and Dietz, "Structure, agency and environment".

25. International Strategy for Disaster Reduction, *Living with Risk. A Global Review of Disaster Reduction Initiatives*, vol. II (Geneva, United Nations, 2004), p. 6.

26. Ibid.

27. Dayton-Johnson, "Natural disasters".

28. Cutter, "Vulnerability to environmental hazards".

29. United Nations Environment Programme (UNEP), *Assessing Human Vulnerability to Environmental Change: Concepts, Issues, Methods and Case Studies* (UNEP, 2003). Available from www.unep.org/geo/GE03/pdfs/AssessingHumanVulnerabilityC.pdf.

30. See T. Cannon, J. Twigg and J. Rowell, *Social Vulnerability, Sustainable Livelihoods and Disasters*. (Kent, University of Greenwich, 2004); and Thywissen, *Components of Risk*.

31. Brooks, Adger and Kelly, "The determinants of vulnerability".

32. United Nations Development Programme (UNDP), *Water Governance in the Arab Region: Managing Scarcity and Securing the Future* (New York, United Nations Development Programme, 2013).

33. ESCWA and BGR, "Inventory of shared water resources in Western Asia" (Beirut, 2013).

34. Food and Agriculture Organization (FAO), Aquastat. Available from www.fao.org/nr/water/aquastat/data/query/.

35. Arab Forum on Environment and Development (AFED), *Impact of climate change on Arab countries* (2009).

36. UNDP, *Water Governance in the Arab Region*; and ESCWA and BGR, "Inventory of shared water resources".

37. UNDP, *Water Governance in the Arab Region*.

38. UNEP, ESCWA and UNDP, "Regional Coordination Mechanism (RCM): Issues brief for the Arab Sustainable Development Report – Climate change in the Arab region" (2015), p. 3.

39. B.O. Elasha, *Mapping of Climate Change Threats and Human Development Impacts in the Arab Region*, Arab Human Development Report, Research Paper Series (New York, United Nations Development Programme, 2010).

40. UNDP, *Water Governance in the Arab Region*.

41. Elasha, *Mapping of Climate Change Threats*.

42. Food and Agriculture Organization (FAO), *Coping with Water Scarcity: Challenge of the Twenty-First Century* (Rome, FAO, 2007).

43. Ibid., p. 8.

44. FAO, Aquastat, 2014. Available from www.fao.org/nr/water/aquastat/data/query/.

45. See Arab Centre for the Studies of Arid Zones and Dry Lands (ACSAD), *Drought Vulnerability in the Arab Region: Drought in Syria, Ten Years of Scarce Water (2000-2010), Case Study* (ACSAD, 2011); and Issam Fares Institute for Public Policy and International Affairs, American University of Beirut (AUB), "Impact of population growth and climate change on water scarcity, agricultural output and food security" (AUB, 2014).

46. ACSAD, *Drought Vulnerability*.

47. FAO, *Coping with Water Scarcity*.

48. Beyond 2015 Campaign, "Population dynamics", p. 7.

49. Brooks, Adger and Kelly, "The determinants of vulnerability".

50. See Organisation for Economic Co-operation and Development (OECD), Development Assistance Committee (DAC), *Poverty and Health: DAC Guidelines and Reference Documents* (Geneva, World Health Organization, 2003); and Department of Economic and Social Affairs, *The Inequality Predicament: Report on the World Social Situation 2005* (New York, United Nations, 2005).

51. W.P. Butz, W. Lutz and J. Sendzimir, "Education and differential vulnerability to natural disasters" (International Institute for Applied Systems Analysis, 2014).

52. K. Dow and others, *Linking Water Scarcity to Population Movements: From Global Models to Local Experiences* (Stockholm, Stockholm Environment Institute, 2005), p. 18.

53. UNFPA and others, *Population Dynamics*.

54. Technical Support Team, "Population dynamics", p. 4.

55. ESCWA, *Population and Development Report Issue No. 6: Development Policy Implications of Age-Structural Transitions in Arab Countries* (E/ESCWA/SDD/2013/2).

56. Technical Support Team, "Population dynamics".

57. Data quoted in International Labour Organization (ILO), *Labour Inspection, Gender Equality and Non-Discrimination in the Arab States: Guide Book* (Beirut, ILO, 2014).

58. ESCWA, *Survey of Economic and Social Developments in the Arab Region 2012-2013* (E/ESCWA/EDGD/2013/3).

59. UNFPA and others, *Population Dynamics*, p. 20.

60. Ibid. See also Beyond 2015 Campaign, "Population dynamics", p. 6.

61. ESCWA (2014) "Conflict in the Syrian Arab Republic: Macroeconomic implications and obstacles to achieving the Millennium Development Goals" (E/EDGD/2014/Technical paper.5), p. 2.

62. Economist Intelligence Unit, "Libya country report" (2015).

**Chapter III**

1. Turner and others, "A framework for vulnerability analysis".

2. See Brooks, Adger and Kelly, "The determinants of vulnerability"; and Y.T. Maru and others, "A linked vulnerability and resilience framework for adaptation pathways in remote disadvantaged communities", *Global Environmental Change*, vol. 29 (September 2014), pp. 337-350.

3. See S. Khan, "Vulnerability assessments and their planning implications: a case study of the Hutt Valley, New Zealand", *Natural Hazards*, vol. 64, No. 2 (December 2012), pp 1587-1607; and Turner and others, "A framework for vulnerability analysis".

4. Twigg and Rowell, *Social Vulnerability*; and Thywissen, *Components of Risk*.

5. World Food Programme (WFP), *The State of Food Security and Nutrition in Yemen: Comprehensive Food Security Survey* (Sana'a, 2012).

6. M. Mundy, A. al-Hakimi and F. Pelat, "Neither security nor sovereignty: the political economy of food in Yemen", in *Food Security in the Middle East*, Z. Babar and S. Mirgani, eds. (New York, Oxford University Press, 2014).

7. R.E. Mitchell, "What the social sciences can tell policy-makers in Yemen", *The Middle East Journal*, vol. 66, No. 2 (Spring 2012), pp. 291-312.

8. United Nations, Department of Economic and Social Affairs, *World Population Prospects: The 2012 Revision* (New York, 2012).

9. United Nations, Department of Economic and Social Affairs, *World Urbanization Prospects: The 2014 Revision* (New York, 2014).

10. Yemen is the only country in the Arabian Peninsula to have signed the Refugee Convention of 1951. See United Nations High Commissioner for Refugees (UNHCR), "Yemen factsheet – November 2013" (2013).

11. J. Kambeck, "Land disputes in Yemen", in *Why Yemen Matters: A Society in Transition*, H. Lackner, ed. (Saqi Books, 2014).

12. United Nations High Commissioner for Refugees (UNHCR), "Yemen country profile". Available from www.unhcr.org/pages/49e486ba6.html.

13. Q. Wodon and others, "Climate change, extreme weather events, and migration: review of the literature for five Arab countries", in *People on the Move in a Changing Climate: The Regional Impact of Environmental Change on Migration*, E. Piguet and F. Laczko, eds. (Springer, 2014).

14. Ministry of Health and Population in Yemen and UNICEF, "Yemen: Monitoring the situation of children and women – Multiple Indicator Cluster Survey 2006" (2008). Available from www.childinfo.org/files/MICS3_Yemen_FinalReport_2006_Eng.pdf.

15. Ibid.

16. The World Bank, *World Development Indicators 2012* (Washington D.C., 2012).

17. H. Lackner, "Water scarcity: why doesn't it get the attention it deserves?", in *Why Yemen Matters: A Society in Transition*, H. Lackner, ed. (Saqi Books, 2014).

18. "Access to an improved water source refers to people with access to at least 20 litres of water per person per day from an improved source, such as piped water into a dwelling, public tap, tube-well, protected dug well, and rainwater collection, within 1 kilometre of the dwelling". WHO/UNICEF Joint Monitoring Programme (JMP) for Water Supply and Sanitation, "Yemen: Estimates on the use of water sources and sanitation facilities". Available from www.wssinfo.org/documents/?tx_displaycontroller[type]=country_files (accessed 2 April 2015).

19. Ibid.

20. Ministry of Health and Population in Yemen and UNICEF, "Yemen" (see footnote 214).

21. C. Ward, *The Water Crisis in Yemen: Managing Extreme Water Scarcity in the Middle East* (London: I.B. Tauris, 2015).

22. Lackner, "Water scarcity".

23. Ibid.

24. See M. Haidera and others, "Water scarcity and climate change adaptation for Yemen's vulnerable communities", *Local Environment*, vol. 16, No. 5 (2011), pp. 473-488; and L. Kasinof, "At heart of Yemen's conflicts: water crisis", *The Christian Science Monitor*, 5 Novermber 2009. Available from http://www.csmonitor.com/World/Middle-East/2009/1105/p06s13-wome.html.

25. United Nations Statistics Division, UNdata: Yemen. Available from http://data.un.org/CountryProfile.aspx?crName=Yemen (accessed 23 October 2014).

26. E. Dickson and others, *Urban Risk Assessments: Understanding Disaster and Climate Risk in Cities* (Washington, D.C., The World Bank, 2012), pp. 179-185.

27. World Food Programme, *The State of Food Security*.

28. M. Madbouly,. "Revisiting urban planning in the Middle East North Africa region", paper prepared for the *Global Report on Human Settlements 2009*.

29. UN-Habitat), *The State of Arab Cities* (see footnote 77).

30. M. Madbouly, *Urban Planning and Management in Sana'a Municipality* (Municipality of Sana'a and the World Bank, 2008).

31. Ibid.

32. M. El-Shorbagi, *Sana'a City Development Strategy: Urban Upgrading Study – Informal Residential Development and Informal Areas in Sana'a* (Municipality of Sana'a, 2008).

33. Ibid.

34. W.M.S. al-Daily, "An exploration of State and non-State actor engagement in informal

settlement governance in the Mahwa Aser neighborhood and Sana'a City, Yemen", PhD Dissertation, Virginia Polytechnic Institute and State University, 2013.

35. See M. al-Waraqi, "Urban planning strategy of Sana'a City based on the present and future requirements", unpublished doctoral dissertation, Sana'a University, 2009; K.G. Ahmed, "Overriding the barriers in front of genuine community participation in urban regeneration projects in the Arab cities: a road map", paper presented at the Proceedings of the Second Workshop on Possible Approaches for Improving Informal Settlement within a National Framework in the MENA Region, Aden, 22-24 October 2007; and El-Shorbagi, *Sana'a City Development Strategy*.

36. See S. Dabbas and T. Burns, "Developing effective policy and planning in Yemen", paper presented at FIG Working Week: Bridging the Gap between Cultures, Marrakech18-22 May 2011; and El-Shorbagi, *Sana'a City Development Strategy*.

37. Al-Daily, "An exploration of State and non-State actor engagement".

38. W.A.F. Mahuob, "Decision of rural households on migration into cities and settlement in slums: the case of Sana'a city, Yemen", Master's thesis, Hogeschool Van Hall Larenstein University of Applied Sciences, 2013.

39. Ibid.

40. Al-Daily and others, "An exploration of State and non-State actor engagement".

41. Ibid.

42. Ibid.

43. M. Haidera and others, "Water scarcity" (see footnote 227).

44. Ibid.; and L. Kasinof, "At heart of Yemen's conflicts: water crisis" (2009) (see footnote 227).

45. Ward, *The Water Crisis in Yemen*.

46. World Food Programme, *The State of Food Security*.

47. UNICEF, "Yemen situation report", May 2014. Available from http://reliefweb.int/sites/reliefweb.int/files/resources/UNICEF%20Yemen%20SitRep%20May%202014.pdf.

48. M. Madbouly, *Urban Planning and Management* (see endnote 30).

49. UNICEF, "Yemen situation report", May 2014.

50. UNICEF, At a glance: Yemen. Database available from www.unicef.org/infobycountry/yemen_statistics.html (accessed 18 March 2015).

51. El-Shorbagi, *Sana'a City Development Strategy*.

52. Ward, *The Water Crisis in Yemen*.

53. Madbouly, "Revisiting urban planning" (see footnote 231).

54. Ministry of Health and Population in Yemen and UNICEF, "Yemen" (see footnote 214).

55. Ibid.

56. C. Ward and others, *Yemen's Water Sector Reform Program: A Poverty and Social Impact Analysis* (Republic of Yemen, GTZ and the World Bank, 2007).

57. Ward, *The Water Crisis in Yemen*.

58. M. Zeitoun, "The political economy of water demand management in Yemen and Jordan: A synthesis of findings", WADImena Water Demand Management Research Series (2009), pp. 29-30.

59. IRIN, "Yemen: Capital city faces 2017 water crunch", 23 March 2010. Available from www.irinnews.org/report/88522/yemen-capital-city-faces-2017-water-crunch.

60. The World Bank, "Implementation completion and results report: Sana'a Basin Water Management Project", Report No: ICR00001482 (2010). Available from http://www-wds.worldbank.org/external/default/WDSContentServer/WDSP/IB/2011/03/08/000333038_20110308224031/Rendered/PDF/ICR14820P0649816B01PUBLIC0317120111.pdf.

61. Ward, *The Water Crisis in Yemen*.

62. Ibid.

63. Ibid.

64. Ibid.

65. Al-Daily, "An exploration of State and non-State actor engagement"; and Mahuob, "Decision of rural households on migration into cities and settlement in slums" (see footnote 244).

66. El-Shorbagi, *Sana'a City Development Strategy*.

67. M. Ababsa, "Changes in the regional distribution of population", in *Atlas of Jordan*, M. Ababsa, ed. (Beirut, Institut français du Proche-Orient, 2013), pp. 257-267.

68. Department of Statistics (Jordan), 2013, Statistical year book 2012, Amman.

69. Jordan, Department of Statistics and ICF International, *Jordan Population and Family Health Survey 2012* (Claverton, Maryland, 2013). Available from https://dhsprogram.com/pubs/pdf/FR282/FR282.pdf.

70. See https://www.adaptation-fund.org/wp-content/uploads/2015/01/Jordan%20Revised%20Fully-developed%20programme%20Proposal-08-31-2014+LOE.pdf, p. 6.

71. Ministry of Water and Irrigation, "Jordan water sector: facts and figures 2013" (Amman, 2013). Available from www.mwi.gov.jo/sites/en-us/Documents/W.%20in%20Fig.E%20FINAL%20E.pdf.

72. See https://www.adaptation-fund.org/wp-content/uploads/2015/01/Jordan%20Revised%20Fully-developed%20programme%20Proposal-08-31-2014+LOE.pdf.

73. N. Barhan, "Is good water governance possible in a rentier State? The case of Jordan" (Center for Mellemøststudier, Syddansk University, 2012).

74. Jordan, Ministry of Water and Irrigation, "Jordan water sector".

75. A.M. al-Rawabdeh and others, "A GIS-based drastic model for assessing aquifer vulnerability in Amman-Zerqa Groundwater Basin, Jordan", *Engineering*, vol. 5, No. 5 (May 2013), pp. 490-504.

76. See https://www.adaptation-fund.org/wp-content/uploads/2015/01/Jordan%20Revised%20Fully-developed%20programme%20Proposal-08-31-2014+LOE.pdf.

77. V. Yorke, "Politics matter: Jordan's path to water security lies through political reforms and regional cooperation". Working Paper, No. 2013/19 (Bern, National Centre of Competence in Research on Trade Regulation, 2013). Available from http://www.wti.org/fileadmin/user_upload/nccr-trade.ch/wp5/working_paper_2013_19.pdf.

78. A. Farishta, "The impact of Syrian refugees on Jordan's water resources and water management planning", Master's thesis, Columbia University, 2014.

79. United Nations and Jordan, Ministry of Planning and International Cooperation, *Needs Assessment Review of the Impact of the Syrian Crisis on Jordan* (Amman, 2013).

80. See https://www.adaptation-fund.org/wp-content/uploads/2015/01/Jordan%20Revised%20Fully-developed%20programme%20Proposal-08-31-2014+LOE.pdf.

81. Jordan, Ministry of Water and Irrigation, "Jordan water sector".

82. M.R. Hamdan and A. Salman, "Impact of irrigation water scarcity on the socio-economics of the agricultural sector and food security in Jordan", in *Food Security Under Water Scarcity in the Middle East: Problems and Solutions*, A. Hamdy and R. Monti, eds. (Bari, CIHEAM Options Méditerranéennes, 2005), pp. 399-407.

83. H. Alsharifa and others, "The fate of Disi Aquifer as strategic groundwater reserve for shared countries" (Jordan and Saudi Arabia), *Journal of Water Resource and Protection*, vol. 3, No. 10 (2011), pp. 711-714.

84. Jordan, Ministry of Water and Irrigation, *Water for Life: Jordan's Water Strategy 2008-2022* (Amman, 2009). Available from http://data.unhcr.org/syrianrefugees/admin/download.php?id=4230.

85. V.I. Grover, A.R. Darwish and E. Deutsch, "Integrated water resources management in Jordan" (Cairo, Economic Research Forum, 2012).

86. J. Yoon, "An integrated assessment of

water resources sustainability in Jordan", doctoral thesis, University of Stanford, 2007.

87. Ibid.

88. Grover, Darwish and Deutsch, "Integrated water resources management in Jordan".

89. Ibid.

90. UNDP, *Water Governance in the Arab Region*.

91. Ibid.

92. Barhan, "Is good water governance possible in a rentier State?".

93. ESCWA, ACWUA and the League of Arab States, "First report on the MDG+ Initiative" (see footnote 27).

94. International Union for the Conservation of Nature (IUCN), presentation to the Athens Groundwater Conference, Amman, 11 July 2014.

95. Jordan, Ministry of Planning and International Cooperation, *National Resilience Plan 2014-2017: Proposed Priority Responses to Mitigate the Impact of the Syrian Crisis on Jordan and Jordanian Host Communities* (Amman, 2014).

96. UNDP, *Water Governance in the Arab Region*.

97. Within that last context, water is pumped from Disi to Amman or from groundwater aquifers to end users.

98. Jordan, Ministry of Water and Irrigation, "Jordan water sector".

99. C. Scott, "Facing water scarcity in Jordan: reuse, demand reduction, energy, transboundary approaches to assure future water supplies", *Water International*, vol. 28, No. 2 (June 2003), pp. 209-216.

100. Jordan, Ministry of Water and Irrigation, "Jordan water sector".

101. United States Agency for International Development (USAID), *Institutional Support and Strengthening Program: Institutional Assessment Report* (Washington, D.C., 2011).

102. Jordan, Ministry of Water and Irrigation, "Jordan water sector".

103. Jordan, Ministry of Planning and International Cooperation, *National Resilience Plan 2014-2017*.

104. Barhan, "Is good water governance possible in a rentier State?".

105. Ibid.

106. UNDP, *Water Governance in the Arab Region*.

107. Ibid.

108. USAID, *Institutional Support and Strengthening Program*.

109. V. Yorke, "Politics matter" (see footnote 229).

110. UNDP, *Water Governance in the Arab Region*.

111. See http://www.fao.org/ag/agp/agpc/doc/Counprof/Jordan/Jordan.htm.

112. UNDP, *Water Governance in the Arab Region*.

113. Hamdan and Salman, "Impact of irrigation water scarcity".

114. Ibid.

115. International Fund for Agricultural Development (IFAD), *The Hashemite Kingdom of Jordan: Country Programme Evaluation* (Rome, 2011), p. 4.

116. D.J. Goode and others, *Groundwater-level Trends and Forecasts, and Salinity Trends, in the Azraq, Dead Sea, Hammad, Jordan Side Valleys, Yarmouk, and Zarqa Groundwater Basins, Jordan* (U.S. Geological Survey, 2013).

117. See www.usaid.gov/jordan/sustainable-agriculture-and-water-management.

118. Grover, Darwish and Deutsch, "Integrated water resources management in Jordan".

119. A.N. al-Shadiadeh, F.M. al-Mohammady and T.R. Abu-Zahrah, "Factors influencing adoption of protected tomato farming practices among farmers in the Jordan Valley", *World Applied Sciences Journal*, vol. 17, No. 5 (2012), pp. 572-578.

120. Jordan, Department of Statistics and ICF International, *Jordan Population* (see footnote 279).

121. Ibid.

122. H.F. al-Qudah, "Land reform impact on socioeconomic factors: the Jordan River Valley", *Jordan Journal of Agricultural Sciences*, vol. 6, No. 2 (2010), pp. 248-260.

123. Ibid.

124. A.E. Sidahmed and others, "Pre-identification mission: support to agricultural development in Jordan", Contract No. 2011/278635 – version 1 (European Commission, 2012).

125. Ibid.

126. V. Yorke, "Politics matter".

127. Grover, Darwish and Deutsch, "Integrated water resources management in Jordan".

128. V. Yorke, "Politics matter".

129. K. Abu-Thallam, "Assessment of drought impact on agricultural resources in northern Jordan Valley", Master's thesis, University of Jordan, 2003.

130. United Nations and Jordan, Ministry of Planning and International Cooperation, *Needs Assessment Review of the Impact of the Syrian Crisis on Jordan* (see footnote 292).

131. Hamdan and Salman, "Impact of irrigation water scarcity".

132. M. Haddadin and M. Shteiwi, "Linkages with social and cultural issues", in *Water Resources in Jordan: Evolving Policies for Development, the Environment and Conflict Resolution*, M. Haddadin, ed. (Washington, D.C., Resources for the Future, 2006).

133. Ibid.

134. Sidahmed and others, "Pre-identification mission".

135. Ibid.

136. Ibid.

137. International Fund for Agricultural Development (IFAD), "Enabling the rural poor to overcome poverty in Jordan" (Rome, 2007). Available from http://www.ifad.org/operations/projects/regions/PN/factsheets/jo.pdf.

138. See https://www.adaptation-fund.org/wp-content/uploads/2015/01/Jordan%20Revised%20Fully-developed%20programme%20Proposal-08-31-2014+LOE.pdf.

139. Ibid.

140. Jordan, Ministry of Water and Irrigation, *Water for Life: Jordan's Water Strategy 2008-2022* (see footnote 297).

141. Jordan, Ministry of Water and Irrigation, *Establishing the Post-2015 Development Agenda: Sustainable Development Goals (SDG) towards Water Security – The Jordanian Perspective* (Amman, 2014).

142. USAID, *Institutional Support and Strengthening Program*.

143. See https://www.adaptation-fund.org/wp-content/uploads/2015/01/Jordan%20Revised%20Fully-developed%20programme%20Proposal-08-31-2014+LOE.pdf.

144. Grover, Darwish and Deutsch, "Integrated water resources management in Jordan".

145. Knowledge and Action Fostering Advances in Agriculture (KAFA'A), *Baseline Assessment: On-farm Water Management, Crop Production and Marketing* (Development Alternatives Inc., 2004). Available from http://www.ncare.gov.jo/OurNCAREPages/PROJECTMENU/RelatedPages/KAFAA/Kafa'a%20assessment/A-11.%20Baseline%20survey.pdf.

146. Jordan, Ministry of Planning and International Cooperation, *National Resilience Plan 2014-2017* (see footnote 309).

147. H. Namrouqa, "Farmers willing to shift to less water intensive crops", *Jordan Times*, 31 May 2012.

148. Scott, "Facing water scarcity in Jordan" (see footnote 313).

149. Jordan, Ministry of Water and Irrigation and Ministry of Planning and International Cooperation, *Report of the High-level Conference on Jordan's Water Crisis*, Amman, 2 December 2013.

150. United Nations and Jordan, Ministry of Planning and International Cooperation, *Needs Assessment Review of the Impact of the Syrian Crisis on Jordan* (see footnote 292).

151. K. Wazani, *The Socio-economic Implications of Syrian Refugees on Jordan: A Cost-Benefit Framework* (Amman, Konrad Adenauer Stiftung, 2014).

152. Ibid.

153. Ibid.

154. Jordan, Department of Statistics and ICF International, *Jordan Population* (see footnote 279).

155. Wazani, *The Socio-economic Implications of Syrian Refugees on Jordan* (see footnote 387).

156. Data from the Ministry of Agriculture of Jordan.

157. Jordan, Ministry of Water and Irrigation and Ministry of Planning and International Cooperation, *Report of the High-level Conference on Jordan's Water Crisis* (see footnote 385).

158. Ibid.

159. Wazani, *The Socio-economic Implications of Syrian Refugees on Jordan*.

160. 2010 data from the Department of Statistics of Jordan.

161. Data from the Ministry of Planning and International Cooperation of Jordan.

162. United Nations and Jordan, Ministry of Planning and International Cooperation, *Needs Assessment Review of the Impact of the Syrian Crisis on Jordan*.

163. UNDP, "Mitigating the impact of the Syrian refugee crisis on Jordanian vulnerable host communities", Jordan Country Project Document (Amman, 2013). Available from http://www.jo.undp.org/content/dam/jordan/docs/Poverty/PD%20Signed%20with%20Japan.pdf.

164. 2010 data from the Department of Statistics of Jordan.

165. 2014 data from the Department of Statistics of Jordan.

166. United Nations and Jordan, Ministry of Planning and International Cooperation, *Needs Assessment Review of the Impact of the Syrian Crisis on Jordan*.

167. Wazani, *The Socio-economic Implications of Syrian Refugees on Jordan*.

168. United Nations and Jordan, Ministry of Planning and International Cooperation, *Needs Assessment Review of the Impact of the Syrian Crisis on Jordan*.

169. Ibid.

170. IDARA (Instituting Water Demand Management in Jordan), "Northern Governorate audit report 2009" (Amman).

171. Grover, Darwish and Deutsch, "Integrated water resources management in Jordan".

172. Ibid.

173. Jordan, Ministry of Planning and International Cooperation, *National Resilience Plan 2014-2017*.

174. USAID, *Institutional Support and Strengthening Program*.

175. Strategic Foresight Group, *The Hydro-insecure: Crisis of Survival in the Middle East* (Mumbai, 2014).

176. S. Greenwood, "Water insecurity, climate change and governance in the Arab world", *Middle East Policy, vol. 21, No. 2* (Summer 2014), pp. 140-156.

177. Jordan, Ministry of Water and Irrigation and Ministry of Planning and International Cooperation, *Report of the High-level Conference on Jordan's Water Crisis*.

178. Mercy Corps, *Tapped Out: Water Scarcity and Refugee Pressures in Jordan* (Oregon, 2014).

179. 2014 data from the Department of Statistics of Jordan.

180. Jordan, Ministry of Planning and International Cooperation, *National Resilience Plan 2014-2017*.

181. OHCHR (2014), End visit statement by the UN Special Rapporteur on the Human Right to Water and Sanitation, March 11-16, 2014.

182. K. Darmame and R. Potter, "Social equity issues and water supply under conditions of 'water stress': A study of low- and high-income households in Greater Amman, Jordan", in *Water, Life and Civilisation: Climate, Environment and Society in the Jordan Valley*, S.J. Mithen and E. Black, eds. (Cambridge, Cambridge University Press, 2011), p. 544.

183. V. Yorke, "Politics matter".

184. P.H. Bakir, "Survey findings of government institutions effort in water, energy, and environment. Final report", Report No. 4, Public Action for Water, Energy and Environment Project (Amman, USAID, 2010), p. 6.

185. Jordan, Ministry of Planning and International Cooperation, *National Resilience Plan 2014-2017*.

186. Ibid.

187. Wazani, *The Socio-economic Implications of Syrian Refugees on Jordan*.

188. UNDP, *Water Governance in the Arab Region*.

189. ACTED and others, *Inter-agency Knowledge, Attitudes and Practices Study of Syrian Refugees in Host Communities in North Jordan* (Amman, 2013).

190. UNDP, *Water Governance in the Arab Region*.

191. A. Baker, "Will Syria's refugee crisis drain Jordan of its water?", *Time Magazine*, 4 April 2013.

192. REACH, *Access to Water and Tensions in Jordanian Communities Hosting Syrian Refugees: Thematic Assessment Report* (Amman, 2014).

193. Baker, "Will Syria's refugee crisis drain Jordan of its water?".

194. UNDP, *Water Governance in the Arab Region*.

195. Strategic Foresight Group, *The Hydro-insecure*.

196. Ibid.

197. OHCHR, End visit statement.

198. L. Hamai and others, *Integrated Assessment of Syrian Refugees in Host Communities: Emergency Food Security and Livelihoods; Water, Sanitation and Hygiene, Protection* (Amman, Oxfam GB, 2013).

199. Office of the High Commissioner for Human Rights (OHCHR), End visit statement by the United Nations Special Rapporteur on the Human Right to Water and Sanitation, Jordan, 16 March 2014. Available from http://www.ohchr.org/EN/NewsEvents/Pages/DisplayNews.aspx?NewsID=14386&LangID=E.

200. H. Bawadi, "Prevalence of food insecurity among women in northern Jordan", *Journal of Health, Population and Nutrition*, vol. 30, No. 1 (2012), pp. 49-55.

201. K. Masharqa, "Embodying the everyday practices of urban water: The discourse of water scarcity and women's subjectivities in Amman, Jordan", Master's thesis, American University of Cairo, 2012.

202. USAID and others, "Community-Based Initiatives for Water Demand Management Project II", presentation made at the Sixth Regional Coordination Meeting of the Water and Livelihoods Initiative, Amman, November 2014. Available from http://www.icarda.org/wli/pdfs/sixthRegionalCoordinationMeeting/Integrating%20Field%20Tested%20Technologies%20into%20Proven%20Methods%20for%20Adoption%20in%20Jordan.pptx.

203. UNDP, *Water Governance in the Arab Region*.

204. Grover, Darwish and Deutsch, "Integrated water resources management in Jordan".

205. D. Swanson and others, "Indicators of adaptive capacity to climate change for agriculture in the Prairie region of Canada", International Institute for Sustainable Development (IISD) Working Paper (Winnipeg, IISD, 2007).

**Chapter IV**

1. R. Warren Flint, "The sustainable development of water resources", Water *Resources Update*, No. 127 (January 2004), pp. 48-59. Available from http://www.eeeee.net/sd_water_resources.pdf.

2. See https://sustainabledevelopment.un.org/topics.